mindful eating

mindful eating

A Guide to
Rediscovering
a Healthy and Joyful
Relationship
with Food

Jan Chozen Bays, MD

FOREWORD BY JON KABAT-ZINN

Shambhala
Boston & London
2009

Shambhala Publications, Inc.
Horticultural Hall
300 Massachusetts Avenue
Boston, Massachusetts 02115
www.shambhala.com

9   8   7   6   5   4   3   2   1

First edition

Printed in the United States of America
♾ This edition is printed on acid-free paper that meets the American National
Standards Institute z39.48 Standard.

♻ This book was printed on 30% postconsumer recycled paper. For more
information please visit us at www.shambhala.com.

Distributed in the United States by Random House, Inc.,
and in Canada by Random House of Canada Ltd

Designed by Barbara Haines

Library of Congress Cataloging-in-Publication Data

Bays, Jan Chozen.
Mindful eating: a guide to rediscovering a healthy and joyful
relationship with food / Jan Chozen Bays; foreword by Jon Kabat-Zinn.—1st ed.
p.   cm.
Includes bibliographical references and index.
ISBN 978-1-59030-531-7 (pbk.: alk. paper)
1. Food habits—Psychological aspects. 2. Compulsive eating. 3. Thoughtfulness.
4. Consciousness—Religious aspects—Buddhism. I. Title.
TX357.B455 2009
394.1—dc22
2008032480

DEDICATION

CONTENTS

FOREWORD

To see a World in a Grain of Sand
And a Heaven in a Wild Flower,
Hold Infinity in the palm of your hand
And Eternity in an hour.

                                   —William Blake

IT IS HARD TO THINK OF a biological function more essential to sustaining our life than eating, since, unlike plants, we don't photosynthesize sustenance out of light and air. Breathing happens on its own, thank goodness. Sleeping too. But eating requires some deliberate engagement on our parts in either growing, gathering, hunting, shopping, going to a restaurant, or otherwise acquiring a range of life-sustaining foodstuffs that often need some kind of preparing and combining by us or others to be maximally beneficial. As mammals, we have complex circuitry in the nervous system to insure that we are motivated to find and eat food (hunger and thirst) and to know when those urges have been satisfied and the body has gotten what it needs for the moment to sustain itself for a time (satiety). Yet, it is all too easy for us in this postindustrial era to take eating so for granted that we engage in it with huge unawareness, and also freight it (all puns intended) with complicated psychological and emotional issues that obscure and sometimes seriously distort a simple, basic, and miraculous aspect of our lives. Even the question of what food really is takes on whole new meanings in an age of industrial agriculture, factory processing, and continual invention of new "snacks" and "foods" that our grandparents wouldn't recognize. And with a huge and sometimes obsessive preoccupation with health and eating in this brave new world, it is equally easy to fall into a certain kind of "nutritionism,"[1] which makes it difficult to simply enjoy food and all the social functions that revolve around preparing, sharing, and celebrating the miracle of sustenance and the web of life within which we are embedded and upon which we depend.

On a parallel note, mind-states of unawareness, addiction, and delusion sadly abound in this world and, we might say, function as equal opportunity destroyers of sanity, well-being, and authentic relationship at every level of the body, mind, and world. Every single one of us suffers from them to one degree or another, not simply around food and eating, but in many different aspects of our lives. It is part and parcel of the human condition, perhaps made worse in this era by the particular stresses and pressures of our nonstop, 24/7 connectivity, attention-deficit hyperactivity, celebrity-obsessed culture. But the good news is that the inner and outer pressures on our minds and bodies and the suffering that comes from these sometimes unhealthy influences can be recognized and intentionally worked with to the benefit of anyone willing to undertake the cultivation of even a bit of mindfulness and heartfulness. This book is a gentle invitation to engage in that healing, and a wise guide to accompany you on the journey of a lifetime into your own wholeness.

Nowhere are the elements of the human condition we call unawareness, addiction, and delusion more poignantly and tragically manifested nowadays than in widespread disregulations and disorders in our relationships to food and to eating. These pathologies of imbalance are driven by many complex factors in society itself. Sadly, they have resulted in cultural norms that support particular brands of delusion, obsession, and endless preoccupation with how much the body weighs. It manifests as a gnawing and pervasive, if sometimes submerged and disguised or overcompensated-for discomfort and dissatisfaction with how one's body looks and how it feels inwardly. This pervasive dissatisfaction nests itself within ordinary concerns about one's appearance, but is compounded by desires to fit in to an idealized model of how one *should* look and the impression one's appearance *should* make on others that shape and trump the authenticity of one's own interior experience. This dissatisfaction in the mind lends itself to pathologies associated with body image, distortions in how one perceives oneself inwardly and outwardly, and with deep issues of self-worth. Catalyzed in large measure by ubiquitous media exposure, it is prevalent even in children and adolescents, and is pervasive across the life span and right into old age. The sadness of it all is immense and needs to be met with boundless compassion and self-compassion, as well as effective strategies for restoring balance and sanity in our world and in our individual lives.

It is well known now that these pathologies of imbalance are manifesting as never before in a number of epidemics in both children and adults, in both males and females. One might say that the entire society suffers from disordered eating in one way or another, just as, from the perspective of the meditative traditions, we suffer from a pervasive attention deficit hyperactivity disorder. As is made clear in this book, the one is intimately related to the other.

One manifestation of our disordered relationship to food and eating is the obesity epidemic of the past twenty-plus years in the United States. This phenomenon is driven by a host of complex factors and compounded by increasingly sedentary lifestyles in adults and children, coupled with a ubiquitous availability of processed foods and by a farming and food industry that is the admiration of the world in some ways, and which runs amok in others.[2] The extent of the epidemic in obesity can be gauged from graphic displays of the rates per state in the United States, starting around 1986.[3] It is now spreading to other countries, particularly in Europe. This epidemic has been driven in part by the phenomenon of supersizing, as so graphically illustrated in the movie *Supersize Me*, in the ever-expanding notion of a reasonable portion size (and even plate size) for one person, by increasing inactivity, and by the endless availability of high-calorie, low-nutrient foods. Many medical schools are developing research and clinical programs to better understand and deal with this growing phenomenon in both adults and children, and some are even reaching out in imaginative collaborations with forward-looking elements of the food and restaurant industries.[4] Clinical programs for children abound.[5]

Another manifestation of our disordered relationship to food and eating is the tragedy of anorexia and bulimia, particularly among girls and young women. These disregulations in eating behaviors are often driven by distortions in self-image and body image, shaped by subterranean and often unacknowledged feelings of shame, inadequacy, and unworthiness. In many, they arise following horrendous but often hidden trauma experiences and histories. In others, they arise as poorly understood but complex reactions to familial, social, and societal dynamics, compounded by the fashion, advertisement, and entertainment industries, an obsession with celebrities, and the sexualization of appearance starting in childhood. Here, any impulses to restrict food intake are life-threatening and need to be met with a huge degree of professional understanding of the tortured web of pain that people can be caught in, huge acceptance and compassion for their suffering, as well as recognition of and unfailing support for the interior strengths they possess but may not recognize, including their potential for healing.

On top of all of these problematic elements in our relationship to food is the even more pervasive disregulation, pointed out earlier, in our relationship to our own lives as they are unfolding in the present moment. It doesn't take much in the way of attention to realize that much of our lives are caught up in a preoccupation with the past and future at the expense of the present moment, the only time any of us ever have to nurture ourselves, to see, to learn, to grow, to change, to heal, to express our feelings, to love, and above all to live. If we are always on the way to someplace else, to some better now, when we will be thinner, or happier, or more accomplished, or whatever it is, then we can never be in wise relationship with this moment and love ourselves as we actually are. This too is a pervasive tragedy . . . that we might miss the actuality of the life that is ours to live because we are so distracted, preoccupied, and driven by attempting to attain some mind-constructed ideal in some other time that is often also, sadly, shaped by unexamined desires, aversions, and illusions. Of course, this has huge relevance in terms of eating and to how we might be in relationship to our bodies and to all the forces that might carry us into these whirlpools of addiction, disregulation, and sorrow. This is a practical choice that we can have a major personal say in, no matter what the rest of the world is doing, thinking, or selling. However, it does require a motivation to break free of deep and longstanding conditioning and habits of unawareness and addiction that weigh us down, sometimes both literally and metaphorically.

What we might characterize as a condition of endemic mindlessness in our society is something we can do something about and take personal responsibility for, as described so effectively in this book in regard to eating and to food in all its guises and manifestations. And who better to offer this path to greater sanity and balance than Jan Chozen Bays, who is a seasoned pediatrician specializing in childhood trauma, a longtime leader of mindful eating groups, and an exceptional mindfulness teacher steeped in an ancient and profound tradition of wisdom and compassion?

Mindfulness is all about paying attention, and the awareness and freedom that emerge from that present-moment gesture of profound relationality and consciousness. It is the antidote to addictive preoccupations and indeed, preoccupations of all kinds that carry us away from the actuality of the present moment. When we start to pay attention in an intentional and nonjudgmental way, as we do when we cultivate mindfulness, and thus bring ourselves back into the present moment, we are tapping into very deep natural resources of strength, creativity, balance, and yes, wisdom—interior resources that we may never have realized we even possess. Nothing has to change. We don't have to be any different or "better." We don't have to lose weight. We don't have to fix any imbalances or strive for any ideals. All we have to do is pay attention to aspects of our lives that we may have been ignoring in favor of various idealizations that have unwittingly carried us further and further from our intrinsic wholeness (the root meaning of the words *health, healing,* and *holy*) that is already here, available to us in this very moment, and in any and every moment, a wholeness that is never not present.

This book emphasizes that, with practice, it is possible to have mindfulness become a reliable foundation for holding and healing one's entire life. This optimistic perspective suggests that if you commit yourself to engaging in this program of bringing greater mindfulness to the whole process of eating, you are taking a major step to giving your life back to yourself, and in the process, freeing yourself from the imprisoning and deadening habits of unawareness, obsession, and addiction in regard to eating, body image, and even more, one's own mind and body and its/their relationship to the world. This engagement has the potential to restore your intrinsic and original beauty, as you befriend yourself as you are. It is an invitation to balance of both mind and body, and to a deep interior satisfaction that goes by the name of happiness, or well-being.

In the Stress Reduction Clinic at the University of Massachusetts, the first formal meditation we usually engage in is to eat one raisin slowly and mindfully. With guidance, it can take up to five minutes or even longer. The clinic participants, for the most part medical patients, don't expect meditation, or stress reduction for that matter, to be associated with eating, and that alone is a useful and cliché-dispelling message that meditation is not what we usually think it is. Actually, anything can be a form of meditation if we are present for our experience, which means if we are wholeheartedly aware. The impact of this strange and somewhat artificial exercise is driven home immediately, just in the seeing of the object we are about to take in, the smelling of it, the observing of how it actually gets to and then into the mouth, the chewing, the tasting, the changes as the raisin disintegrates, the impulse to swallow, the swallowing, the resting quietly for a moment in the aftermath of it all, all held in an exquisite awareness that seems to come effortlessly. People exclaim: "I don't think I have ever *tasted* a raisin before." "This is amazing." "I actually feel full." "I feel warm." "I feel whole." "I feel calm." "I feel peaceful." "I feel like a nervous wreck." "I hate raisins." (There are a lot of different responses, and no right answers—just what people are experiencing.)

But just like Blake's grain of sand and his wild flower, you can see the entire world in one raisin, hold the universe and all life in the palm of your hand, and then, of course, in your mouth too, as it soon becomes a source of nurturance on so many different levels, energy and matter and life itself enlivening and replenishing the body, the heart, and the mind. And in community no less, in this instance, since there may be thirty or more people in the room, all new to mindfulness, all newcomers to this eight-week clinical program we call MBSR, or mindfulness-based stress reduction. One raisin can teach you a lot.

You will find this raisin exercise, and many more, in this book. If you give yourself over wholeheartedly to the practices described here with a certain degree of discipline and commitment, yet leavened with kindness and gentleness so that you cut yourself enough slack not to force things to conform to some ideal, I am sure that you will be thanking yourself and Dr. Bays for recovering your life and for enjoying the blessings of food in ways that feel liberated and delighted.

JON KABAT-ZINN
Professor of Medicine Emeritus
University of Massachusetts Medical School
Stress Reduction Clinic
Center for Mindfulness in Medicine, Health Care, and Society

September 2008

Notes

1. Michael Pollan, "The Age of Nutritionism: How Scientists Have Ruined the Way We Eat," *New York Times Magazine*, January 28, 2007.
2. For an interesting discussion of this issue, see for example Michael Pollan, *The Omnivore's Dilemma: A Natural History of Four Meals* (New York: Penguin Press, 2006).
3. See for example www.cdc.gov/nccdphp/dnpa/obesity/trend/maps/.
4. See for example www.healthykitchens.org.
5. See for example the Optimal Weight for Life (OWL) clinic at Children's Hospital in Boston, a multidisciplinary center for the diagnosis and management of overweight children; and David Ludwig, *Ending the Food Fight: Guide Your Child to a Healthy Weight in a Fast Food/Fake Food World* (Boston: Houghton Mifflin, 2008).

PREFACE

I AM WRITING THIS BOOK to address an increasingly widespread and unnecessary form of suffering. Our struggles with food cause tremendous emotional distress, including guilt, shame, and depression. As a physician, I've also seen how our eating problems can lead to debilitating diseases and even to premature death.

According to the U.S. Department of Health, nearly two out of three American adults are overweight or obese. It's also estimated that millions of Americans suffer from anorexia or bulimia. One could call this an epidemic of "eating disorders," but I prefer to think of the problem as an increasingly unbalanced relationship to food. One of the primary causes of this imbalance is a lack of an essential human nutrient: mindfulness. Mindfulness is the act of paying full, nonjudgmental attention to our moment-to-moment experience. This book explores how we can use mindfulness to free ourselves from unhealthy eating habits and improve our overall quality of life.

Right now we're in need of a fresh approach to our eating problems, because the conventional methods aren't working. Research shows that no matter what diet people undertake, no matter what kinds of food they stop or start eating, they lose an average of only eight to eleven pounds and then gain it back in about a year. Only a few individuals are successful in losing a significant amount of weight and not regaining it. We can see that dieting is not the answer.

We've also tried to solve our weight problems by altering the food we eat in the hope that we could continue to eat in an unbalanced way without any ill effects. We have removed the calories, the fat, the sugar, and the salt. We have added protein, vitamins, fiber, artificial fat, and chemical sweeteners. This war on food has meant increased revenues for companies that create processed food, but it has not altered our expanding waistlines or brought us back to a wholesome way of eating.

Another approach has been to wage war on the fat in our bodies through starvation diets, compulsive exercise, or liposuction. Fat cells are actually trying their best to help us. Their job is to keep us warm and to provide emergency fuel for lean times. We can remove fat cells through surgery, but if we continue to consume extra calories, new fat cells will grow in a dutiful attempt to fulfill their role as energy storage containers.

We've tried attacking the body in other ways as well. Most large hospitals have opened departments of bariatric medicine to provide weight loss surgery and the aftercare it necessitates. These operations reduce the size of the stomach or bypass parts of the gut to produce malabsorption. With a smaller stomach, people experience pain, nausea, and other kinds of discomfort if they eat more than one-half to one cup of food at a time. Following malabsorption surgery people may suffer chronic diarrhea and have to take many supplements to avoid becoming malnourished. There is no question that surgery helps people lose weight and reverse side effects such as diabetes. However, it appears that several years after undergoing surgery, many patients regain weight, with only one in ten stabilizing at their target weight. Hundreds of thousands of people each year are undergoing this surgery, which is expensive (at least $25,000) and risky (as of this writing one in a hundred patients die and one in ten have serious complications, often requiring further surgery). The cost of this treatment alone makes it unavailable to most people.

After undergoing bariatric surgery, people are forced to change their eating habits. They must eat mindfully or suffer acute discomfort. However, many patients eventually learn to "eat around" the restrictions imposed by altered intestinal anatomy, and they gain weight again. It appears that a significant number of patients develop "transfer addictions" after surgery, substituting alcohol, compulsive gambling, shopping, or sex for food.

If dieting or surgery are not practical treatments for adults, they certainly will not work for the 20 percent of American children who are now overweight or obese. Until about ten years ago, we pediatricians seldom saw overweight children in our clinics. Now they are common, as are serious complications including diabetes. Some researchers are predicting that this generation will live shorter life spans than their parents because of disordered relationships to food and eating. We do not want to push young children into neurosis about diet and obsession with weight. We need a new approach.

Similar challenges arise in trying to treat those whose weight becomes dangerously low due to anorexia or bulimia. Medical treatment, including hospitalization, intravenous nutrition, and dripping liquid nutrition into feeding tubes, often results in weight gain that is only temporary.

The situation is clear. The developed countries are in the midst of a serious epidemic of disordered relationships to food and eating. We are in urgent need of a treatment that will work equally well for children and their parents. We are in urgent need of a treatment that is inexpensive or free and can be used by anyone. It should at least be without negative side effects. Ideally it would have positive side effects.

The best treatment would be one that could be started with initial guidance and education by professionals but would be easy and interesting enough to be continued long-term by people on their own. The treatment should be accessible to people of all ages and social conditions, including children. It should have an immunizing effect, preventing children from developing full-blown eating problems. It should provide strong support to those who are undergoing medical treatment or surgery. Ideally this treatment would cause long-lasting changes and result in a permanent cure.

Mindfulness is the only treatment that I know of that fits this description. Mindfulness addresses our disorder at its source. The problem is not in our food. Food is just food. It is neither good nor bad. The problem is not in our fat cells or stomach or small intestine. They are just trying quietly to do their job. The long-term solution is not to eat food that has been stripped of nutrition or to mutilate healthy organs or to deliberately produce a second serious disease, malabsorption. The source of the problem lies in the thinking mind and the feeling heart. Mindfulness is the perfect tool for the delicate operation of laying open the inner workings of these two most essential organs. Mindfulness is the perfect catalyst for setting into motion the course of their complete healing.

This book was inspired by the enthusiasm generated by the mindful eating retreat we give at the Zen monastery where I live and teach. Of our many workshops and retreats this one seems to generate the highest level of excitement and appreciation for the power of mindfulness to shed light upon a most vital aspect of life, even in people with little experience with meditation. When mindful eating is ignored, it causes pervasive and unnecessary suffering. When mindfulness is applied to eating, a world of discovery and delight opens. This is a world that has been hidden, quite literally, beneath our noses.

It is my sincere wish that this book will help you to open yourself to the joy and delight, the richness and splendor, of the simple acts of eating and drinking, so that you can find true, deep, and lasting satisfaction with food and enjoy eating throughout your life.

ACKNOWLEDGMENTS

MANY THANKS to all the students who have educated and entertained me—and each other—in our mindful eating classes and workshops, and especial thanks to those whose stories (names changed to protect the guilty) are included in this book.

To Freiderike Eishin Boissevaine, MD, and Megrette Fletcher, RD, whose enthusiasm about the potential for mindful eating to relieve the suffering of their patients provided clarity when I lost perspective about exactly why I was holed up for weeks with a keyboard and a glowing screen.

To Brian Wansink, who has done the most devious and ingenious experiments to provide empirical support for the insights we've had in mindful eating classes. Though I've never met him, I picture Brian along with his research assistants in their lab at Cornell, slapping their thighs and guffawing as they discuss an idea for a new experiment, and then falling to the floor, rolling around, weak with laughter, as they share the results.

Many thanks also to Ajahn Amaro of Abhayagiri Monastery, who fielded, with his characteristic equanimity and wry humor, my many e-mail questions about sources in the Pali canon and how the Buddha ate.

To the editors at Shambhala Publications, who had the courage to try out a very different kind of dharma book. May your faith be rewarded, if not here, then with many merit points to be redeemed in the hereafter.

mindful eating

1 | What Is Mindful Eating?

THIS BOOK IS WRITTEN for all those who would like to improve their relationship to food. Whether you have a moderate tendency to overeat, as so many of us do, or whether you are struggling with obesity, bulimia, anorexia, or other such problems, this book is for you.

I am a doctor (my specialty is pediatrics), and I am also a longtime Zen teacher. At the heart of Zen, and of the Buddhist tradition in general, is the practice of mindfulness. Over my many years practicing medicine, and many years of practicing mindfulness and teaching it to others, I have come to trust mindfulness as one of the very best medicines.

Most books and techniques for changing our eating try to impose change from the outside. Sometimes this fits with the unique being that we are and it works. Sometimes it doesn't. Mindfulness brings about change from the inside. A natural and organic process, it occurs in the manner and at the rate that fits us. It is the ultimate in natural healing.

What Is Mindfulness?

It is not necessary to become a Buddhist or attend a weeklong silent retreat in order to experience the benefits of mindfulness. Mindfulness is an ability we all possess and can cultivate. Recently mindfulness has become a popular concept, increasingly accepted and studied in the worlds of science, healthcare, and education. When mindfulness remains only a concept, however, it has little use in our lives. When it is learned and used, it becomes a powerful tool for us to awaken to the full potential of our life.

> Mindfulness is deliberately paying attention, being fully aware of what is happening both inside yourself—in your body, heart, and mind—and outside yourself, in your environment. Mindfulness is awareness without judgment or criticism.

The last element is key. In mindful eating we are not comparing or judging. We are simply witnessing the many sensations, thoughts, and emotions that come up around eating. This is done in a straightforward, no-nonsense way, but it is warmed with kindness and spiced with curiosity.

Mindfulness is rooted in the realization that when we ignore what we are seeing, touching, or eating, it is as if it does not exist. If our child or partner comes to talk with us and we are distracted and not listening, we all go away feeling hungry for connection and intimacy. If we eat while watching television, distracted and not really tasting, the food goes down without our noticing it. We remain somehow hungry and unsatisfied. We go away from the table searching for something more to nourish us.

Through mindful eating we can learn to be present when we eat. It seems so simple, to be aware of what we are eating, but somehow we have lost track of how to do it. Mindful eating is a way to reawaken our pleasure in simply eating, simply drinking.

The Zen master Thich Nhat Hanh has called mindfulness a miracle. It seems like it. When we learn how to use this simple tool and find for ourselves what it can do, it seems miraculous. It can transform boredom into curiosity, distressed restlessness into ease, and negativity into gratitude. Using mindfulness we will find that anything, *anything*, we bring our full attention to will begin to open up and reveal worlds we never suspected existed. In all my experience as a physician and a Zen teacher I have never found anything to equal it.

A large and growing body of scientific studies supports the claims about the surprisingly reliable healing abilities of mindfulness. Dr. Jon Kabat-Zinn at the University of Massachusetts Medical School has developed a curriculum that draws on mindfulness-based stress reduction (MBSR). He first taught MBSR techniques to people suffering from chronic pain and disease, people whose doctors had referred them as a last resort after other medical therapies had failed. The results were so good that he expanded his research to other illnesses. Other doctors and therapists learned MBSR techniques and tried it out successfully with a variety of disorders. There are now many articles in medical and psychology journals documenting the benefits of MBSR in illnesses ranging from asthma to psoriasis, heart disease to depression.[1]

The Joy of Mindful Eating

Mindful eating is an experience that engages all parts of us, our body, our heart, and our mind, in choosing, preparing, and eating food. Mindful eating involves all the senses. It immerses us in the colors, textures, scents, tastes, and even sounds of drinking and eating. It allows us to be curious and even playful as we investigate our responses to food and our inner cues to hunger and satisfaction.

Mindful eating is not directed by charts, tables, pyramids, or scales. It is not dictated by an expert. It is directed by your own inner experiences, moment by moment. Your experience is unique. Therefore you are the expert.

Mindful eating is not based on anxiety about the future but by the actual choices that are in front of you and by your direct experiences of health while eating and drinking.

Mindful eating replaces self-criticism with self-nurturing. It replaces shame with respect for your own inner wisdom.

As an example, let's take a typical experience. On the way home from work Sally thinks with dread about the talk she needs to work on for a big conference. She has to get it done in the next few days to meet the deadline. Before starting to work on the speech, however, she decides to relax and watch a few minutes of TV when she gets home. She sits down with a bag of chips beside her chair. At first she eats only a few, but as the show gets more dramatic, she eats faster and faster. When the show ends she looks down and realizes that she's eaten the entire bag of chips. She scolds herself for wasting time and for eating junk food. "Too much salt and fat! No dinner for you!" Engrossed in the drama on the screen, covering up her anxiety about procrastinating, she ignored what was happening in her mind, heart, mouth, and stomach. She ate unconsciously. She ate to go unconscious. She goes to bed unnourished in body or heart and with her mind still anxious about the talk.

The next time this happens she decides to eat chips but to try eating them mindfully. First she checks in with her mind. She finds that her mind is worried about an article she promised to write. Her mind says that she needs to get started on it tonight. She checks in with her heart and finds that she is feeling a little lonely because her husband is out of town. She checks in with her stomach and body and discovers that she is both hungry and tired. She needs some nurturing. The only one at home to do it is herself.

She decides to treat herself to a small chip party. (Remember, mindful eating gives us permission to play with our food.) She takes twenty chips out of the bag and arranges them on a plate. She looks at their color and shape. She eats one chip, savoring its flavor. She pauses, then eats another. There is no judgment, no right or wrong. She is simply seeing the shades of tan and brown on each curved surface, tasting the tang of salt, hearing the crunch of each bite, feeling the crisp texture melt into softness. She ponders how these chips arrived on her plate, aware of the sun, the soil, the rain, the potato farmer, the workers at the chip factory, the delivery truck driver, the grocer who stocked the shelves and sold them to her.

With little pauses between each chip, it takes ten minutes for the chip party. When she finishes the chips, she checks in with her body to find out if any part of it is still hungry.

She finds that her mouth and cells are thirsty, so she gets a drink of orange juice. Her body is also saying it needs some protein and something green, so she makes a cheese omelet and a spinach salad. After eating she checks in again with her mind, body, and heart. The heart and body feel nourished but the mind is still tired. She decides to go to bed and work on the talk first thing in the morning, when the mind and body will be rested. She is still feeling lonely, although less so within the awareness of all the beings whose life energy brought her the chips, eggs, cheese, and greens. She decides to call her husband to say good night. She goes to bed with body, mind, and heart at ease and sleeps soundly.

About This Book

This book is a manual for learning mindfulness while eating. Mindfulness is skill that anyone can develop. It can be applied to anything that arises in our life. It does not depend upon our age, gender, IQ, muscle strength, musical or any other talent, or our ability with foreign languages. As with any skill, developing mindfulness *does* require practice, diligent practice, over a significant period of time. Unlike some types of learning, however, such as learning to play the violin, mindfulness brings immediate rewards. With mindfulness, we can even eat foods we don't particularly like and discover something useful in the process.

This book is not about diets or rules. It is about exploring what we already have and appreciating everything we are doing. Will you lose or gain weight if you bring mindfulness into cooking and eating? I don't know. What you could lose is the weight of the mind's unhappiness with eating and dissatisfaction with food. What you could gain are a simple joy with food and an easy pleasure in eating that are your birthrights as a human being.

We all have to eat. It is a basic requirement of being alive. Unfortunately there are few daily activities that are so loaded with pain and distress, with guilt and shame, with unfulfilled longing and despair than the simple act of putting energy into our bodies. When we learn to eat mindfully, our eating can be transformed from a source of suffering to a source of renewal, self-understanding, and delight.

Much in this book has to do with opening our awareness of our body and mind. When we are able to fully appreciate the basic activities of eating and drinking, we discover an ancient secret, the secret of how to become content and at ease. The Zen teachings talk about the exquisite taste of plain water. Have you ever been very, very thirsty? Maybe you were on a long hike, or sick, or working without a break in the summer heat. When you were finally able to drink, even plain water, you remember how wonderful it was. Actually, each sip of liquid and each bite of food can be that fresh and delicious, once we learn again just to be present.

Mindful eating is a way to rediscover one of the most pleasurable things we do as human beings. It also is a path to uncovering many wonderful activities that are going on right under our noses and within our own bodies. Mindful eating also has the unexpected benefit of helping us tap into our body's natural wisdom and our heart's natural capacity for openness and gratitude.

In the Zen tradition we practice bringing skillful attention, curiosity, and inquiry to all of our activities, including the activities of tasting and eating. The Zen teachings encourage us to explore the present moment fully, asking ourselves questions like:

Am I hungry?
Where do I feel hunger? What part of me is hungry?
What do I really crave?
What am I tasting just now?

These are very simple questions, but we seldom pose them. This book will help you find answers to some of these questions and will give you tools to continue to discover answers in the future.

Mindfulness Is the Best Flavoring

As I write this I am eating a lemon tart that a friend gave to me. He knows how much I love lemon tarts, and he occasionally brings them to me from a special bakery. After writing for a few hours I am ready to reward myself with a tart. The first bite is delicious. Creamy, sweet-sour, melting. When I take the second bite, I begin to think about what to write next. The flavor in my mouth decreases. I take another bite and get up to sharpen a pencil. As I walk, I notice that I am chewing, but there is almost no lemon flavor in this third bite. I sit down, get to work, and wait a few minutes.

Then I take a fourth bite, fully focused on the smells, tastes, and touch sensations in my mouth. Delicious, again! I discover, all over again (I'm a slow learner) that the only way to keep that "first bite" experience, to honor the gift my friend gave me, is to eat slowly, with long pauses between bites. If I do anything else while I'm eating, if I talk, walk, write, or even think, the flavor diminishes or disappears. The life is drained from my beautiful tart. I could be eating the cardboard box.

Here's the humorous part. I stopped tasting the lemon tart because I was thinking. What was I thinking about? Mindful eating! Discovering that, I have to grin. To be a human being is both pitiful and funny.

Why can't I think, walk, and be fully aware of the taste of the tart at the same time? I can't do all these things at once because the mind has two distinct functions, thinking and awareness. When the thinking function is turned up, the awareness function is turned down. When the thinking function is going full throttle, we can eat an entire meal, an entire cake, an entire carton of ice cream, and not taste more than a bite or two. When we don't taste what we eat, we can end up stuffed to the gills but feeling completely unsatisfied. This is because the mind and mouth weren't present, weren't tasting or enjoying, as we ate. The stomach became full but the mind and mouth were unfulfilled and continued calling for us to eat.

If we don't feel satisfied, we'll begin to look around for something more or something different to eat. Everyone has had the experience of roaming the kitchen, opening cupboards and doors, looking vainly for something, anything, to satisfy. The only thing that will cure this, a fundamental kind of hunger, is to sit down and be, even for a few minutes, wholly present.

If we eat and stay connected with our own experience and with the people who grew and cooked the food, who served the food, and who eat alongside us, we will feel most satisfied, even with a meager meal. This is the gift of mindful eating, to restore our sense of satisfaction no matter what we are or are not eating.

Common Misperceptions

People get confused about mindfulness. They think that if they just do one thing at a time, like eating without reading, or if they move *veeerrry* slowly and carefully, they are being mindful. We could stop reading, close the book, and then eat slowly but still not be mindful of what we are eating. It depends upon what our mind is doing as we eat. Are we just eating or are we thinking and eating? Is our mind in our mouth, or somewhere else? This is a crucial difference.

As we begin to practice mindfulness it does help a lot to slow down and to do only one thing at a time. In fact there are two essential aspects of becoming mindful as we eat. They are slowing down and eating without distractions. As we become more skilled in being present, we can be mindful and speedy. In fact we discover that when we are moving quickly we need to be much more mindful. To be mindful means to have the mind full, completely full, of what is happening *now*. When you're chopping vegetables with a large sharp knife, the faster you slice, the more attentive you have to be, if you want to keep your fingers!

It's also important to understand that mindful eating includes mindless eating. Within the wide field of mindfulness we can become aware of the pull toward mindless eating and notice when and how we slip into it. We can also decide, according to this situation and time, how we're going to approach eating. Part of my work as a doctor involves testifying in court cases as an expert witness. Maybe I'm on the way to court and I haven't had time for lunch. I know it will be hard to stay clear on the witness stand and that court is unpredictable. I may be there for hours. I mindfully decide to undertake mindless eating and order a veggie burger from a fast-food window to eat in the car, trying to at least be mindful about not spilling the special sauce on my one good suit. Mindfulness gives us awareness of what we're doing and, often, why we're doing it.

Establishing a Healthier Relationship with Food

When our relationship to food falls out of harmony, we lose our innate enjoyment of eating. When the relationship has been disordered for many years, it is easy to forget what "normal" eating is like. Actually it's what "normal" eating *was* like, because in infancy almost everyone experienced a natural happiness with eating and an instinctive awareness of how much was satisfying.

Here are some elements of a healthy relationship to food.

1. You feel happy and fully engaged in life when you are not eating. (Food is not your only reliable source of pleasure and satisfaction.)
2. If you are not feeling hungry, you don't eat.
3. You stop eating when you feel full and are able to leave food on the plate.
4. You have intervals of at least several hours when you are not hungry or thinking about food, punctuated by (meal) times when you do feel hungry and take enjoyment in eating.
5. You enjoy eating many different kinds of foods.
6. You maintain a healthy weight that is steady or fluctuates within a range of five to seven pounds. You don't need to weigh yourself more than once every few months or years.
7. You don't obsess about food or count calories in order to decide if you can "afford" to eat something or not.

If some or all of the items on this list don't apply to you, you're not alone. Many of us have developed unhealthy habits due to a variety of influences in our lives. (We'll explore this more in chapter 3.) Fortunately, mindful eating can help restore your natural sense of balance, satisfaction, and delight with food.

About the Exercises and Audio CD

It can be hard to look straight into something that is a source of embarrassment and self-criticism. However, looking straight into our struggles with food is the only way to see through them and find our way out the other side.

The exercises presented in this book are drawn from the mindful eating exercises, workshops, and retreats I've led over the past two decades. Some people (including me) find it difficult to read the instructions for an exercise at the very same time they are trying to *do* the exercise. For this reason we have included an audio CD of guided instructions. The CD contains recordings of the most important mindful eating exercises. I recommend that you begin by reading the book, pausing to try the guided exercises when they are presented in the text, rather than beginning this work by going directly to the CD.

It is not easy to work entirely by yourself on this most vital issue of eating. It might be helpful to find a partner or to form a group to read this book and try the exercises together. In our workshops, after we complete an exercise, we discuss what we experienced and discovered. These discussions can be funny, touching, sad, and revealing. A sense of warm kinship and support builds as we discover that we are not alone in our struggles. You will find a study guide for using the book in a class or group setting at www.mindfuleatingbook.com.

It's important to actually *do* the exercises, especially those that are included on the audio CD. Mindful eating is not theoretical. It cannot be accomplished by reading a book. Mindful eating is based upon experience. Only an actual experience makes the truth alive in our bodies and heart. I could tell you many times how valuable mindful eating can be, but it cannot be satisfying to you until you try it. There's a Zen saying about not trying to satisfy hunger with a painting of a rice cake. The only way to satisfy your body's hunger is to eat the rice cake. The only way to satisfy the hunger in your heart and mind is to eat the rice cake with mindfulness.

Finally, anything that we attend to carefully and patiently will open itself up to us. Once we are able to apply the power of a concentrated, focused mind, anything, potentially all things, will reveal their true hearts to us. It is that heart-to-heart connection with ourselves, with our loved ones, and with the world itself that all of us so dearly long for. It can be found in such a simple act as eating a piece of bread. All it takes is a little bit of courage and the willingness to begin the most delightful of all adventures, the journey of looking, smelling, tasting, and feeling.

EXERCISE

The Basic Mindful Eating Meditation

Now our journey begins. This first mindful eating exercise is essential—many of the other exercises in this book rest upon this one, so *please don't skip it.* In this exercise we will experiment with bringing our full awareness to eating a very small amount of food. It is best to have someone read this exercise aloud to you, one step at a time. You'll find a recording of this exercise on the audio CD, track 2.

Preparation: For this exercise you will need a single raisin. Other foods will also work, such a dried cranberry, a single strawberry, a cherry tomato, or an unusual type of cracker.

1. Begin by sitting quietly and assessing your baseline hunger: How hungry are you, on a scale of zero to ten? Where do you "look" in your body to decide how hungry you are?

2. Imagine that you are a scientist on a mission to explore a new planet. Your spaceship has landed and found the planet to be quite hospitable. You can breathe the air and walk around without any problem. The surface of the planet seems to be bare dirt and rock, and no one has seen any obvious life forms yet. The food supplies on your spaceship are running low, however, and everyone is getting hungry. You have been asked to scout out this planet to look for anything that might be edible.

As you walk around you find a small object lying on the ground, and you pick it up. Place the raisin (or other food item) on your palm. You are going to investigate it with the only tools you have, your five senses. You have no idea what this object is. You have never seen it before.

3. *Eye hunger*   First you investigate this object with your eyes. Look at its color, shape, and surface texture. What does the mind say that it could be? Now rate your eye hunger for this item. On a scale of zero to ten, how much hunger do you have for this object based upon what your eyes see?

4. *Nose hunger*   Now you investigate it with your nose. Smell it, refresh the nose, and sniff it again. Does this change your idea of whether it might be edible? Now rate nose hunger. On a scale of zero to ten, how much hunger do you have for this object based upon what your nose smells?

5. *Mouth hunger*   Now you investigate this object with your mouth. Place it in your mouth but *do not bite it.* You can roll it around and explore it with the tongue. What do you notice?

   Now you can bite this mysterious object, but only once. After biting it once, roll it around again in the mouth and explore it with the tongue. What do you notice?

   Now rate mouth hunger. On a scale of zero to ten, how much hunger do you have for this object based upon what the mouth tastes and feels? In other words, how much does the mouth want to experience more of it?

6. *Stomach hunger*   Now you decide to take a risk and eat this unknown object. You chew it slowly, noticing the changes in the mouth in texture and taste. You swallow it. You notice whether there are still any bits in the mouth. What does the tongue do when you have finished eating it? How long can you detect the flavor?

   Now rate stomach hunger. Is the stomach full or not, satisfied or not? On a scale of zero to ten, rate stomach hunger. In other words, how much does the stomach want more of this food?

7. *Cellular hunger*   Become aware of this food passing into the body. Absorption begins as soon as we begin chewing. Are there any sensations that tell you that this food is being absorbed? How is it being received by the cells in the body?

  Now rate cellular hunger. On a scale of zero to ten, how much would the cells like to have more of this food?

8. *Mind hunger*   Can you hear what the mind is saying about this food? (Hint: Often the mind talks in "shoulds" or "should nots.") Now rate mind hunger. On a scale of zero to ten, how much would the mind like you to have more of this food?

9. *Heart hunger*   Is the heart saying anything about this food? On a scale of zero to ten, how soothing or comforting is it? Would the heart like you to have more of this food?

You might like to repeat this exercise with liquid. Pick a drink you have never had before, such as an exotic fruit juice. Take your time and assess each kind of thirst separately.

_____

At first we might find this exercise difficult. As with all aspects of practice, the more you do it, the more your awareness opens up. If you try this exercise with many kinds of food and drink, gradually you will be able to sense and rate the different kinds of hunger more easily. As you continue to practice mindful eating you will develop skill and confidence in a new and more balanced relationship with food. You will be able to nourish the body, heart, and mind, and to regain a sense of ease and enjoyment with eating.

One of the essential aspects of mindful eating is that of becoming more inquisitive and interested in the feeling of hunger itself. In the next chapter, we will explore the seven kinds of hunger that we touched on in this exercise.

2 | The Seven Kinds of Hunger

MINDFULNESS WITH EATING begins at the beginning, with hunger. You may have heard the famous Zen question, "What is the sound of one hand [clapping]?" In mindful eating we might ask, What is the sound of hunger? What is the taste of hunger? Where does hunger reside in the body? What causes hunger to arise?

There is also a Zen saying, "When hungry, just eat." It sounds simple, but it's not. For most of us, when we were children it actually *was* that simple. Studies show that infants and young children have an intuitive sense of what and how much to eat. When babies are given a variety of foods on the tray of their high chairs, to their parents' dismay, they may eat only one food and ignore all the rest. Their mother may despair, thinking, "How will they grow up healthy if all they eat is mashed potatoes?" If researchers are able to convince the mother to relax, wait, and watch, they can show her that over the course of a week her baby will eat just right, as if prompted by an inner nutritionist. Babies are tuned in to the messages from their body. Given enough choices and time they will eat in a balanced way, just the right amounts of calories, vitamins and minerals, proteins, fats, and carbohydrates. This is a skill, an inner listening, that we all were able to do at one time but forgot as we grew older.

Have you watched healthy young children eat? They run in from a morning of playing hard, sit down at the table, and with obvious appetite they eat just enough. Then off they run to play again. Maybe they had to be called several times to come in and eat. Meals are short but necessary refueling stops in between times of play. Eating is secondary to the business of being a child.

As these intuitive eaters grow older, eating is no longer a fueling stop. Food begins to serve many purposes. It is used to sooth, to distract, to procrastinate, to numb, to entertain, to seduce, to reward, and even to punish. The once straightforward relationship between hunger, eating, and satisfaction of our childhood becomes tangled up in all sorts of thoughts and emotions.

As adults we may find that we have to call ourselves *away* from dinner and coax ourselves *not* to eat. The business of eating has become a primary focus, an over-the-kitchen-counter medicine for the many pressures and anxieties of our busy lives. Our eating has become driven by many different forces, many kinds of hunger.

What happened as we grew into adults that turned our natural hunger and our easy ways of finding satisfaction in eating into complicated problems? The answer has two parts. First, our environment taught us unhelpful habits related to eating and food. Then our minds took over from our bodies. The intelligence we had as infants disappeared under pressure from our anxious caretakers. As their affection for us morphed into anxiety about us, our innate wisdom about eating and our innocent pleasure in eating began to fade away. Out of love for us they ruined our natural appetite.

Perhaps your father's family was poor and there was pervasive anxiety in his childhood home about whether there would be enough food on the table tomorrow. Your dad resolved that his kids would never go without, and thus he takes pride in serving steak every Saturday night. He told you, "When I was kid we were lucky to have any meat at all. There are plenty of children dying because they don't have food, so eat your steak!" Never mind that you didn't like meat, or that your leftover steak could not be sent airmail to Africa, or that your parents had served you too much food. You felt guilty for not being able to obey your parents, for not appreciating what they had worked so hard to give you, and for eating while watching the faces of starving people on the evening news.

In restaurants the pressure grew stronger. "I paid good money for this food, so you better eat it all!" The habit you developed in your childhood of cleaning your plate may have saved you a lot of grief then. But it can *cause* you a lot of grief if it persists into middle age. Unless you are a lumberjack or an Olympic swimmer, cleaning your plate in a restaurant these days can easily fill you with twice the calories you can burn in a day. Portion sizes for many foods in restaurants are two to five times larger now than they were when our parents went out to eat.

Here's another example. Let's say you reacted to your parents' loving nagging by rebelling. Let's say they told you not to drink coffee because it would stunt your growth, or that you must eat your vegetables before you had dessert. You decided that as soon as you left home you would drink coffee and eat desserts any time you felt like it. That kind of bouncing off of what your parents pushed you to do is called a reactive habit pattern. You leave home thinking, "Finally I'm free," but you are not. When our behavior is controlled by reactive habit patterns from childhood, we are still tethered to our parents. We are not free.

Mindfulness practice has the potential to free us from the reactive habit patterns we carry around inside. It can liberate us from the unwanted voices and emotions that have taken over our eating and flavored our food, obscuring its taste and depriving us of our birthright, which is to simply eat and enjoy it thoroughly.

The Zen teachings encourage us not to worry about who started all this anxiety and guilt, or who is to blame for our unwholesome habit patterns around food. We say that these kinds of difficulties are a normal part of growing up as a human. Everyone gets bumped and scraped and injured as they grow up. You needn't look around outside or inside yourself for someone to blame.

The question we *are* interested in is, can we change it? If so, who can change it? The answer to the first question is yes. It is possible, through the power of awareness, to unfreeze reactive habit patterns and shift in a very natural way toward health. Who can change it? Only you. You, just as you are. You do need a certain amount of courage to look directly at what is going on in each moment. You have that courage, or you wouldn't have read this far in this book. You also need the support and encouragement of others who have decided to get on with the work of changing, too.

All of us want to move toward greater freedom, but the experience of freedom does not occur overnight. Often we overchallenge ourselves, as when making New Year's resolutions. This results in frustration and more critical inner voices. We can get off to a good start by lowering our standards and initiating our mindful eating by having one conscious sip of tea in the morning. Take a moment to become aware of the color of the tea, its fragrance. Feel the liquid in your mouth and throat. Open your awareness to the presence of warm sunlight, cool rain, and dark earth in this one sip of tea. Everything will unfold from this simple act. Just being aware for a few moments seems like a small event. Don't underestimate the power of mindfulness. It is through these small moments of mindfulness that we reverse old habits and initiate an inner movement toward health.

Why Do You Feel Like Eating?

Before we work on mindfulness during eating, we need to become aware of what urges us to eat. Most people will tell you they eat because they are hungry. When you ask them to describe how they know that they are hungry, however, they become befuddled.

One of the reasons people are confused about hunger is that there are several different types of hunger. All of these types are actual experiences. They occur as sensations, thoughts, and even emotions within our bodies, minds, and hearts.

There can be many reasons for the feeling "I am hungry." It could be that we have not eaten for two days. Perhaps we are tired or anxious or lonely. Some of our experiences of hunger are not hunger for food, but when we feel them, we mistakenly try to relieve them by eating. With mindfulness we can begin to untangle and separate these different experiences of hunger. Only then can we respond to each one in an appropriate and wholesome way.

The most basic type of hunger is physiologic. It is the request of our body for food. It occurs when our energy reserves are low and our cells ask for more fuel to keep us warm and alive. For example, when we are cold our bodies need calories to burn to keep us warm. Typically we become hungrier in the winter and put on a few pounds of insulating fat. In hot weather we lose our appetites, eat lightly, and keep cooler by shedding a few pounds. If we were able to perceive and respond just to cellular hunger, in the way wild animals do, we would feed ourselves in a sane and straightforward way. When hungry we would just eat. When not, not. Life would be simple.

The beauty of being a human is that we are made up of more impulses than those needed for bare survival. We take delight in food. It calls to us through our senses, our eyes, our sensitive nose, our watering mouth, our longing heart. When our senses are activated, we often respond in an automatic way, by putting food into our mouths. In order not to be fooled, in order to create some space for the possibility of change, we need to look carefully at what is happening inside our own being. We need to investigate our own experiences of different kinds of hunger. We need to insert a tiny moment of reflection before we bite into a hot slice of pizza or the gooey chocolate brownie. This sounds easy, but it can be an interesting challenge.

This chapter explores the kinds of hunger we have discovered in our mindful eating workshops. They are eye hunger, nose hunger, mouth hunger, stomach hunger, cellular hunger, mind hunger, and heart hunger. In addition to these seven, there is hunger that is actually thirst. After we learn to tune in to these different kinds of hunger, we can sit down and do a quick assessment before eating: On a scale of one to ten, what is my level of eye hunger? Of mouth hunger? Of cellular hunger? Once we know this, we can eat appropriately and satisfy all the parts of us that are hungry. We can thoroughly enjoy eating.

Eye Hunger

You have just finished a large meal with a small group of friends in a restaurant.

The atmosphere has been happy and warm, the food delicious. The waitress approaches and asks, " May I show you the dessert tray?" You start to protest, "No, I'm really stuffed," but find yourself saying instead, "It can't hurt to look." The tray appears. The eyes roam over an appealing array, a fresh Meyer lemon tart with a flower of whipped cream on top, a dark chocolate mousse with ginger shavings, a thick slice of apple pie oozing caramel filling, New York cheesecake in raspberry sauce . . . Hmmm . . .

Even though the stomach is protesting, "I'm too full. Please, no more!" the eyes are enchanted (and it's hard to send the expectant young waitress back without an order). The decision is no longer whether to have a dessert but which dessert to have. Eye hunger has won out. The eyes say, "I could eat that!" even when stomach and cellular hunger are oversated.

Advertisers know about eye hunger. They devise lovely food ads in magazines, on billboards, on TV, and on movie theater screens. There are photographers whose specialty is photographing food so as to maximize its allure through the eye portal. The eye sees, the eye clings, the eye sends signals to the mind saying, "We're hungry for that!" The eye can convince the mind to override the signals from the stomach and body, even when they are not at all hungry.

After a good dinner in the restaurant you and your friends decide to go to a movie. As you settle into your seats, brilliant ads for food and drink shine down upon you from the huge screen: Raisinets, Good & Plenty, Butterfingers, cheese nachos, hot buttered popcorn, Coke and Pepsi. You've just eaten, but the sight of the caramel dripping from a three-foot Snickers bar causes eye hunger to kick in. The mind agrees. The movie will be two hours long, and besides, there's always room for a Snickers.

Or maybe you decide that you don't have room for any more food. Your friend, however, buys a large popcorn and, just to be polite, passes it to you. It smells so good. You have a choice, to sniff deeply and just enjoy the smell ("weird!") or to start munching ("normal").

People generally decide how much of a given food they will eat based upon feedback from the eyes. The eyes say something like, "Let's eat half of this" or "Let's eat all of this." In his book *Mindless Eating: Why We Eat More Than We Think*, Brian Wansink describes research showing that people who are given a large bucket of free but stale popcorn will dip in twenty-one more times and eat 173 more calories than people given a medium-sized bucket. This happens regardless of whether they have just eaten a full meal or not. In other words, the eyes will override information from the mouth ("This stale popcorn tastes like styrofoam") and from the stomach and body ("We just ate, give us a break"). The ears are coconspirators. It hard to listen to other people in the theater around you munching away and resist the desire to join in.[1]

Researchers wanted to see how far the power of the eyes to override other signals of satiety could be stretched. They invented the bottomless soup bowl, which continuously refilled as people ate. After twenty minutes of eating, the people with bottomless bowls still had not detected that this was occurring! Even though the people with bottomless bowls ate 73 percent more soup than people with normal bowls, they estimated that they had eaten the same amount of calories as everyone else.[2]

The eyes also have the power to override the mouth. In *Mindless Eating* Wansink tells the story of a Navy cook whose troops were demanding cherry Jell-O. He had none on hand but found that he was able to make them believe they were eating cherry Jell-O simply by adding red food coloring to lemon Jell-O.[3]

Even the experts, the people who do this very research, can be fooled by the eye. At a party they served themselves and ate significantly more ice cream, without being aware of it, if they were given larger serving scoops and larger bowls. If we turn this around, the power of eye hunger can be turned to good use. People wishing to eat less should use smaller plates or bowls and smaller serving utensils. They can fill their plate up, but at least half the plate should be filled with vegetables and salad, the other half with protein and starch.[4] The mix of colors and shapes satisfies eye hunger, the variety of tastes and textures satisfies mouth hunger, and the balance of nutrients satisfies cellular hunger.

The eye can even make us hungry when it reads words about food. When I was first married, I was fresh out of college. Wanting to study how to be a wife and cook, I read *The Joy of Cooking*, which my grandmother had given me as a wedding present. As I read, I became hungry. My mouth watered as I took in not actual food but *words* about food, words that conjured up images of delicious dishes. I began cooking my way through the book. I also ate my way through it. I planned meals beginning with the dessert and working backward. I was a person who never weighed myself because my weight was always the same—but now I noticed that my clothes were not fitting. My husband commented that I was looking *zaftig* (Yiddish for "pleasantly plump").

Along with the difficulty of tight clothing, I began to be secretive. While my husband was at work, I would bake, say, a pan of fudge brownies. That night after dinner we each would have one or two. The next day, when he went off to work, I would sample the rest, and continue sampling until they were all gone. Afraid that he would notice, and feeling guilty about eating four days' dessert at once, I would bake another pan. Then I would "have to" eat two to four brownies more so the pan would look the same as it had the night before.

At this point I realized that I was in trouble. When I did find a scale, I discovered that I had gained fifteen pounds. I realized that I was eating not from hunger but from a mixture of boredom and frustrated creativity. I got a job, became busy, and gradually went back to my accustomed size. I also gained a healthy respect for the suffering of people who struggle with eating.

EXERCISES

Becoming Aware of Eye Hunger

When you first sit down to eat, take a few moments to look at the food. Notice colors, textures, shapes, arrangements on the plate. What do the eyes like about the food?

Buy or borrow a women's magazine such as *Woman's Day* or *Martha Stewart Living*.

Leaf through the pages, noticing what pictures appeal to eye hunger. How many photos in one magazine made you hungry?

If there are recipes in the magazine, try reading some without paying attention to the pictures. (It is hard to ignore the photos. They make them appealing on purpose.) This may work better if you have someone else read the recipes out loud. Notice if just hearing the recipes creates hunger for you or not.

When you go to a restaurant notice anything that appeals to your eye hunger. Include the menu and any food displays in your investigation.

SATISFYING EYE HUNGER

What satisfies eye hunger? Beauty. Remember this common experience of eye hunger: You've eaten a filling meal and then the dessert tray arrives. If those desserts were blended in one bowl, a muddy mélange of pureed cheesecake, apple strudel, chocolate mousse, and lemon meringue pie, you'd say no thanks. It's the deliberate eye appeal, the beauty of each dessert, that persuades you to take in the extra calories.

To satisfy eye hunger we have to ask, what is beautiful?

The Japanese are masters of the art of nourishing through the eyes. In a traditional formal meal there are often twelve or fifteen small courses, each one a work of art appropriate to the season. Each offering is described by the waitress in a quiet, lilting voice. First she brings a little bowl of clear soup with a few twists of citron peel and fragrant herb leaves, then a bit of freshly made tofu with a pungent miso dressing, grilled and resting on fern leaves, followed by a pine-scented matsutake mushroom on a yellow and orange maple leaf. As each handmade bowl or plate is cleared away, another small treasure arrives: a delicately carved fresh bamboo shoot, a few slices of baked yam, a quivering square of sesame tofu, each with its own sauce and exquisite decoration.

You can sit for several hours, like a king or queen, receiving many small works of art, presented one at a time so each can be fully appreciated. You leave satisfied, completely nourished through all the senses, and warmed in your heart by the loving attention that is palpable in all you have eaten.

Our eyes do get hungry. When we are distracted and not really looking at things, we feel vaguely dissatisfied and disconnected. Think of yourself rushing off to work. You run by your child or partner and give them a quick good-bye peck on the cheek. This habit, of not really looking, of skimming our eyes over the surfaces of things, leaves us hungry and lonely in a fundamental way. When we stop and look with awareness, we connect. A brief connection like this can lift our mood, feeding our heart for hours. When we *just look*, anything we see becomes beautiful: cracks in a sidewalk, a dead plant, the wrinkled hands of an old woman. The Navaho admonish their people, "Walk in beauty." When we use mindful eyes, everything is beautiful and everyone walks in beauty.

EXERCISE

Creating a Feast for the Eyes

Try making a mindful meal once a week for yourself as if you were a guest. You could get out your best plates and silverware, a place mat or tablecloth, even a small vase of flowers and a candle. Arrange food appealingly, as if for a guest. As you eat, let your eyes "feed" on not only the food but the other aspects of your table.

In mindful eating classes we serve apples on two different plates. The first plate is picked to be unattractive and it holds a few less-than-perfect apples. The second plate has apple slices carefully arrayed on a bed of leaves and flowers. People rate each for eye hunger. (In Japan people do not eat whole apples or pears. They are always sliced and attractively presented.)

Feeding Eye Hunger without Eating

As you proceed through this book, you'll learn to observe your hunger with greater curiosity and attentiveness. Sometimes you'll discover that when you feel hungry, it's not that your body wants food but that your eyes are hungry for beauty.

Experiment with feeding eye hunger by itself, without eating any food. Find something that is lovely or at least interesting to look at. Stop and really look at this something for a few minutes, drinking it in with your eyes. It could be the colored petals of a flower, a picture on the wall, or the many greens of the tree leaves outside your office window. Flower gardens or fabric stores are great places to feed the eyes on colors, patterns, and textures. The thing you choose to look at could be as simple as the colored paint on the walls or the patterns and textures of a cement sidewalk.

Imagine that the energy that radiates from this sight enters your eyes and is absorbed into your body. Feed your eyes as long as you like. You may find that feeding the eyes also feeds the heart.

Nose Hunger

I had a sudden and powerful awareness of nose hunger when the doors of the airport shuttle train opened. We'd had a sixteen-hour flight, stuffed into small seats with no chance to exercise, lulled through the sleepless hours by six mediocre movies and airline meals at times that did not match our bodies' desire for food. With a tendency toward constipation on long sedentary trips, I landed feeling tired, out of sorts, and uncomfortably full. I was roused abruptly from half sleep when the smell of hot spicy tomato sauce drifted in through the open doors of the train. "I smell pizza! Let's have some pizza!" my mind yelled.

Fortunately the messages from the rest of my body were very clear. "Are you crazy? You are not convincing the mouth up there to take in one more morsel until we get rid of what's plugging up the works down here." The smell of food had awakened a desire for "comfort food," food that actually would increase the suffering of my poor uncomfortable body. It was more evidence that disharmony with food begins with lack of awareness within the body, heart, and mind.

Smells exert a primitive and potent effect upon the subconscious mind. Maybe it's because the olfactory nerves are just short outgrowths from the brain, or because the sense of smell was so important to our ancestors. They depended upon their sense of smell to locate food and to distinguish friends from enemies in forests or the dark of night. A good sense of smell was protective, indicating what foods might be good to eat and giving warning when food had spoiled. Humans are not the best smellers in the animal kingdom, but we are still able to distinguish ten thousand different smells.

What we call the "taste" or "flavor" of a food is almost entirely the *smell* of the food. Our tongues are actually able to taste only five flavors: sweet, salty, sour, bitter, and amino acids (a protein-like taste). Have you ever lost your sense of smell when you had a bad cold? If you love to eat it can be very distressing. When we can't smell food, we perceive it as having almost no taste. Without smell all the subtlety of flavor is lost. Food becomes something you have to eat because your body needs fuel. You might as well save money and time by eating dog kibble. It's interesting at those times to pay attention to what you are able to detect, which is only the tongue's five basic flavors. The only other characteristic that you notice is in the textures of different foods, soft or crunchy. Just five flavors and a few textures are not enough to interest us.

Merchants are very aware of nose hunger, and they count on it to entice you. Think of the smells of a bakery, a coffee shop, a fast-food hut, or a cinnamon bun stand that pipes that almost irresistible smell all over the mall. The right smells will make us eat more. When researchers impregnated plastic bowls with the artificial odor of cinnamon and raisin, people ate more plain oatmeal than when the bowls were scented with a discordant scent, macaroni and cheese.[5] I can't eat chocolate anymore, but when I serve, say, chocolate truffles, I'll hold one, inhale deeply, and just enjoy the aroma. It's almost as good as eating it.

EXERCISE

Becoming Mindful of Nose Hunger

This is not an exercise to do when eating in polite company (unless you want to get rid of your polite company). Wait until you are alone or with someone you can explain this to.

1. Before you start to eat a meal, smell the food. Rather than bending down to nuzzle your food, bring the plate or bowl or piece of food up to your nose and inhale deeply, like a wine connoisseur. Do this several times, trying to detect as many components of the smells as you can. You can imagine that you have been asked to guess the ingredients or to write a description of the aroma.

2. As you eat, continue to be aware of smell (which we also call taste). As you chew, notice if the taste is stronger on the in-breath or the out-breath, or does it change?

3. After you've finished eating, sit for a few moments and notice how long you continue to taste the food. If you decided not to take another bite until you could no longer taste the food you had just swallowed, how long might that take?

SATISFYING NOSE HUNGER

Nose hunger is satisfied by fragrance. Once we asked my Zen teacher Maezumi Roshi why we offered incense four times a day as part of our services. Instantly he replied, "Because it is food for the ancestors. Those who have died have no bodies. This fragrance is what nourishes them." My scientific mind was a little stunned, but my practice mind took this information in and I have contemplated and used it while doing mindful eating ever since.

Feeding Yourself with Fragrance

This is a lovely, subtle meditation on breath and smell. As you breathe, maintain awareness of changes in scent on the in- and out-breath. To be aware of the changing flow of smell is a more delicate and difficult meditation than to be aware of changes in what the other senses take in, such as sound or touch.

You might like to begin this practice in a setting where scent is fairly obvious. It could be a meditation room where incense is burning or at a shopping mall suffused with the smell of cinnamon buns. If your sense of smell is not good, you could try meditation on the smells at a food court or in your meditation space at home when someone is cooking dinner.

Once you have some practice with ongoing awareness of obvious smells, try the meditation on scent out of doors, preferably at night, when you are not as distracted by visual phenomena.

This is a fairly radical exercise. Imagine that you have entered a realm of existence (perhaps after death) in which you have no body, only sensory input and consciousness. You are nourished only by scent. "Feed" yourself by putting something with a pleasant scent in a small bowl or cup, like a teaspoon of vanilla, or almond flavoring, or a bit of spice like nutmeg or cinnamon. Inhale the fragrance, imagining as vividly as you can that it is nourishing you.

What do you notice? Are there any changes in body, heart, or mind as you inhale?

You can also try this with incense, flowers, or aromatic herbs like lavender. You can also sniff your baby's head or lie next to your partner at night and inhale their fragrance, feeling it nourish you. I remember my little sister sitting on the radiator and holding our cat when she was upset. She would calm herself by sniffing its head. She said it smelled like popcorn.

Mouth Hunger

Mouth hunger is the mouth's desire for pleasurable sensations. What constitutes pleasant sensations in the mouth varies from person to person. I don't like hot sauce. If food is fiery hot, my mouth is in such distress it can't taste anything but HOT! If I'm eating Thai shrimp curry with mangoes it might as well be sautéed lumps of clay if it's smothered in chilis. My husband, however, loves hot sauces of all kinds. He says that the sensation of burning in his mouth enhances the flavors of food.

What your mouth experiences as pleasant depends upon factors such as genetics, food habits in your family of origin, cultural traditions, and conditioning, which means the association of certain foods with other pleasant or unpleasant experiences. Strawberries and cream will have an entirely different appeal if you enjoyed them with a lover or if you had to eat them at Grandma's house when you were carsick.

An example of a genetic factor in mouth hunger is the reaction of different people to the herb cilantro. Most people enjoy this green herb in Mexican or Asian food. However, about 10 percent of the population, usually people of European origin, find it revolting. They describe it as tasting like soap, unwashed hair, burned rubber, or crushed bugs. Some people's mouths delight in cilantro, while other people's mouths are dismayed. This appears to be a heritable trait.

Here's another example. There is a curious tropical fruit called durian. It smells like raw sewage. The odor is so strong that people have been kicked off buses for carrying a ripe durian. Some people are able to get past the smell and really enjoy its taste. There are even durian addicts. The mouth's ability to enjoy durian may be a genetic trait, a learned behavior, or both.

I've learned a lot about cultural differences in mouth hunger by traveling abroad. When I lived in Africa there was palpable excitement in the open food market when a certain seasonal delicacy appeared. People crowded around mounds of brown deep-fried nut-like objects, buying them by the cupful and savoring them out of hand as they strolled away from the busy vendor. Infected with their enthusiasm I crowded in close, money in hand, and bought a small bagful. Once at home I discovered that I had purchased half a pound of fried termites! I ate one, then gave the rest to our pet bush baby, who devoured them with relish. I felt queasy about eating fried insects, but the bush baby and the Bantu savored them. However, when the African villagers found out that we ate crayfish and lobster, they thought we were demented. No human beings should eat such things, they told us. The difference between what we each think is delicious or revolting is largely due to conditioning. It depends upon what we were taught was good to eat and drink by our family and culture.

There is an American advertisement for food that promises "a party in the mouth." Like the parties of youth, a party in the mouth seems to consist of full-volume, blasting sensation. In America the food industry has amped up the level of sensation in food, particularly snack foods, to include more salt, more sugar, more spice, and more fat—even more sourness. This is quite noticeable when you travel abroad. In Japan and Europe the soft drinks, teas, and juices have about half the level of sweetness of comparable American drinks. The drinks actually refresh, rather than leaving a cloying stickiness in the mouth. Dessert in Japan is light, usually fresh fruit.

Japanese fruit is grown for taste, not, as in the West, for durability during mechanical picking and long-distance shipping. Fruit in Japan is eaten in season and ripe. The subtle layers of flavor in June strawberries, July melons, August peaches, and September grapes is a new experience for Americans.

People who grow up in cities may never eat fresh-picked fruit and do not know how it is supposed to feel or taste. The woman who owns the local fruit stand near our home told us that she was amazed to see young people put down soft, ripe peaches with distaste. They picked hard "green" peaches even when she told them they were not ripe yet. She was astounded to see them biting into a crunchy peach as they left the store. It seems that a generation has grown up eating green, flavorless, but very durable peaches from the supermarket. These young people are being conditioned to dislike soft, juicy, tree-ripened fruit.

In addition to less sugar, there is also much less fat in Japanese food than we are used to. Your lips are never greasy after dinner in Japan. Animal fat was unpalatable to fresh-fish-eating Japanese at first, and in the old days Westerners were called a derogatory name that meant "stinks like butter." Traditional Japanese food has so little fat that you don't need dishwashing soap. You can wash dishes in plain water. My first Zen teacher did not allow us to wash his dishes with soap because, even when we rinsed well, he could taste the soap residue in his food.

A student who grew up in Philadelphia told me that she disliked cherries when she was a child. When she was older and had fresh cherries for the first time she was surprised. "Wait a minute," she thought, "I like these things! These can't be cherries." She suddenly realized that it was artificial cherry flavor that she disliked. Real cherries actually tasted good. A generation is growing up also thinking that the various "fruit flavors" of jelly beans and Kool-Aid are the true flavors of blueberries, grapes, apples, watermelon, and cherries. I wonder if there will come a time when real fruit will no longer satisfy and only the candy substitute will do?

What the mouth demands is partly dependent upon conditioning. The mouth can be trained to enjoy durian, termites, artificial cherry flavoring, and more or less sugar in juice.

To truly experience "a party in the mouth," we don't need stronger flavoring but the presence of awareness. To satisfy the mouth's hunger for sensation, it isn't enough to put food into the mouth, chew it, and swallow it. *If we want to feel satisfied as we eat, the mind has to be aware of what is occurring in the mouth. In other words, if you want to have a party in the mouth, the mind has to be invited.*

Let's say that you've just sat down to enjoy a bowl of pasta with your favorite sauce. The first bite tastes so delicious! So does the second bite. You comment on the seasoning, and then begin a conversation with your friend about the best restaurants you have eaten in and the best pasta dishes you've had. Suddenly you look down and see that the plate is empty! What happened to that wonderful pasta? After a few bites you didn't taste it, because you were busy talking. Instead of eating the food before you in this moment, this mouthful, you were thinking about memories of food from the past. The mouth's hunger has not been satisfied. The mouth asks for a second helping. It's still hungry. If you talk or watch TV while eating this second helping, you might feel oddly unsatisfied once again, and need a third helping.

This is mindless eating. We all do it. We can all learn to change it. Even a small change, a few minutes of mindful eating each day, can begin a change that will bring us to a different way of experiencing the world around and within us.

By the time we have a third helping, the stomach is groaning. The mouth, however, could still be demanding more sensation, more food. If you had been able to eat in silence, undistracted, with the mind "in the mouth," one helping might have been just enough. The key to satisfying mouth hunger is to be present at the party in the mouth. This means to place the focus of our mind in our mouth and to open our awareness to all the textures, movements, smells, sounds, and taste sensations of eating and drinking.

EXERCISES

Becoming Aware of Mouth Hunger

During the day, notice mouth hunger. How does the mouth signal you, "Please put something in here"? What are the sensations of mouth hunger? See if you can ask the mouth what it wants and why. Does it want something salty, sweet, sour, crunchy, or creamy?

Before you eat, with the food in front of you, pause. Look at the food and become aware of the mouth's desire for food. Rate the mouth's hunger on a scale of zero (no mouth hunger) to ten (my mouth is ready to consume anything).

During the meal, pause every five minutes to assess mouth hunger. Does it change?

Note: It is easier to keep track of mouth hunger if you are not doing anything else during the meal such as talking, reading, or watching TV.

When the mouth seems hungry, look inward to see if the mouth could be thirsty instead of hungry. Even if your mouth says it's hungry, you might try a drink of water, juice, or tea and see if the amount of mouth hunger changes.

When you drink, try holding the liquid in your mouth and savoring it before swallowing.

In other worlds, don't gulp. You can swish it around quietly as if rinsing your teeth, if that helps you to hold and taste each mouthful.

SATISFYING MOUTH HUNGER

Mouth hunger is satisfied by sensation. The mouth is a sensation junkie, an organ of pure desire. We were born with a mouth that desired food. Without it we would have died. The mouth desires variety, variety in flavor and texture. If we are not aware of what is happening in the mouth, the mouth feels chronically deprived and convinces the hand to keep feeding it more.

The mouth is easily bored. It has difficulty staying present with sensations as we continue to chew, as the intensity of flavor begins to fade, and the texture turns to mushy. When the mouth is bored, it asks for another bite. If we keep shoveling in bite after bite, and ignore the signals of "full" coming from the stomach, we will take in more food than our body needs.

If our mouth becomes accustomed to always being stimulated, it won't be happy being empty. We will begin to snack continually, putting food and drink into the mouth during the entire time we are awake. When we eat mindlessly, we pay attention, perhaps, to the first few chews of the first bite. We shove another forkful in before we've even swallowed the first. We look down and are surprised to find that the food has disappeared while we weren't even "looking." When we eat mindfully, we are paying attention to the constant changes in the mouth that make up variety. Even when the food is simple, such as oatmeal and milk or a few potato chips in a bowl, when the guests of honor arrive, Awareness and Curiosity, the dullest event becomes a very interesting party.

Explore the role of texture in feeding mouth hunger. Try eating the same food pureed or whole. For example, you could eat and compare a half cup of unsweetened applesauce with a whole raw apple. Both have the same calories. Which satisfies more?

Try eating a potato chip plain and a second one dipped in water. Which satisfies more?

Chewing can also be an important part of satisfying mouth hunger. Begin by rating mouth hunger on a scale of zero (not hungry at all) to ten (famished). Then eat a few bites of food, chewing each bite at least fifteen or twenty times. If you do not usually chew your food well, you will need to give yourself some extra time. Now rate hunger again. What do you find?

There is a wonderful meditation on just the tongue. I won't describe it here, but you can find it on the last track of the audio CD.

Stomach Hunger

What signals does your stomach give you when it is hungry? For some people hunger is an empty feeling in the abdomen, an emptiness that demands to be filled. Others experience constriction, as if the stomach is trying to grind up food that isn't there. Waves of constriction and relaxation called peristalsis do pass across the smooth muscles of our stomach. Not many people describe these sensations as pleasant.

From the evolutionary point of view, it's good that we perceive "hunger pangs" as unpleasant. If we didn't, we might starve to death. Because these sensations are uncomfortable, we feel an unhappy urgency about doing something to relieve them. Often hunger is described as gnawing, as if an animal were eating at our insides. It growls and complains until we throw food down the tunnel to placate it.

However, the notion that the stomach tells us when we must feed it is not correct. We actually tell the stomach when to be hungry. This occurs through our eating habits. When we eat three meals a day at regular times, the stomach becomes conditioned to expect food at those times. It will growl if we don't feed it according to the schedule we gave it. If we travel to a different time zone the stomach learns to growl at a new time. People who never eat breakfast don't have hunger pangs in the early morning. People who do, do.

If you fast for over three days, the hunger pangs and growling disappear. The abdomen feels flat, quiet, and comfortable. This tells us that stomach hunger is not a permanent, solid feature of our lives, one whose urging we must obey. It's our body hunger that is more fundamental and important to learn to feel.

On the other hand, if we ignore sensations of hunger, we'll get in trouble too. We have to walk the middle way with hunger. This means to be aware of signs of hunger in the whole body, not just the hunger signals from a stomach that demands food at the same time every day. It means not to be upset if our stomach is growling but we can't eat right away or we need to eat less. It also means not ignoring our body when it tells us it needs quality fuel.

This sounds complicated, but with mindfulness to guide us, it's not. It's a matter of learning to "listen" to the body with the inner ear.

There are two areas of potential confusion regarding signals of stomach hunger. Gastroesophageal reflux (GER) is the medical name for what most people call heartburn. It is a disorder in which acid from the stomach moves up into the esophagus and causes irritation. It can occur if we put pressure on the stomach or turn upside down right after a meal. (Don't try sit-ups or headstands after dinner.) Certain foods also can trigger pain coming from the esophagus, especially spicy food or caffeine. If people experience GER symptoms and mistake them for hunger, they may eat more, thinking it will relieve the pain. It can have just the opposite effect, causing more stomach acid to be released and more reflux from the back pressure of overfilling the stomach, thus aggravating the symptoms. An unfortunate cycle begins: feeling discomfort, eating, feeling more discomfort, and eating more.

The same kind of confusion can occur with anxiety, which often makes our stomach growl or grind. If we mistake anxiety for stomach hunger, we may eat, trying to make the growling or gnawing go away. Unfortunately, eating doesn't work. In fact it can start another vicious cycle. That is, when we are worried about something, our stomach signals distress, which we mistake for hunger, which leads us to eat. We then feel more anxious about all that we have eaten that we didn't really need, and our stomach acts up even more. We eat again, thinking it will help, but it just further feeds the guilt and shame, heightening our emotional discomfort, and thus the cycle of needless distress continues.

I find myself in the middle of this cycle when I am working hard to meet a deadline. Anxiety makes me reach for snacks, which I stuff in mindlessly because I'm too busy to take a proper break. I don't taste the snacks because I'm distracted with the work, so my stomach ends up full of junk food and my brain fogs over. This makes me more tense, which triggers further stomach symptoms. I grab for more food.

The cure is to sit down and take care of myself in the proper way. I assess hunger in the eyes, mouth, and stomach. I acknowledge that my stomach is helping me by signaling my anxiety. I thank it for its message and promise to attend to my real needs. I put my feet up for a moment (if only in my mind) and have a slow cup of tea, or peel an orange and eat each bite slowly. I take a short nap or walk outside for a few minutes, feeding my eyes on the many colors of green.

I return, refreshed by the short pause, having stepped off the cycle of trying to treat worry and other uncomfortable emotions in the mind by filling my poor stomach with food.

In our workshops on mindful eating we have found that many people are completely unaware of stomach hunger. They are mystified about how to go about assessing the experience of their stomach and cannot get a read on whether their stomachs are full, half full, or empty. It is a revelation for many people to find that they can begin to "listen" to the stomach and act upon its intelligence. When we are able to do this, very often we find that we are about to put food into a stomach that actually is not hungry, a stomach that asks us to wait for a while and reassess for hunger in a few hours. It is a good feeling to begin to live in harmony with our body, to learn from its wisdom.

Medical scientists are realizing that the digestive system is rich in nerves, so rich that they are speaking of it as a "second brain" in the abdomen. The Japanese have known this for a long time. They have an expression, *haragei*, which means "stomach wisdom." In mindful eating we learn to pay attention to the intelligence of our gut.

EXERCISES

Becoming Aware of Stomach Hunger

Be aware of the sensations in the "stomach" during the day. How does the "stomach" signal to you that it is "hungry"?

- Be aware of any sounds, internal feelings of pressure or movement, warmth or coolness, and so forth, that are signaling hunger.
- When you're eating, what sensations tell you that the stomach is empty? Pleasantly full? Overfull?
- Are there other situations besides hunger that make the stomach feel pangs or discomfort? What do you think is going on at those times?
- When does the stomach signal hunger? Is it at predictable times? When during the day does it signal most strongly: before breakfast, at noon, afternoon, before dinner, or at bedtime?

When you feel hungry, delay eating for a while. Simply be aware of the sensation you call "hunger." Be aware of body sensations, feelings, and thoughts. Is it difficult or easy to feel hunger and deliberately delay eating?

SATISFYING STOMACH HUNGER

What satisfies stomach hunger? The right amount and kinds of food. When you open your awareness to investigate when the stomach is most at ease, what do you find? I find that my stomach likes to do its work. It doesn't like the feeling of being very full. The stomach can't work well when it is overfilled. Although my mouth might enjoy being full most of the time, my stomach disagrees. It likes to be comfortably full, about two-thirds full. It also likes to be empty and to rest.

EXERCISE

Staying Aware of Stomach Hunger during a Meal

When you sit down to eat, take a few seconds to assess stomach hunger on a scale from zero to ten, zero being not hungry and ten being "starving."

After you've eaten half your food, stop eating and take a few seconds to assess stomach hunger again.

At the end of the meal, assess stomach hunger again. To satisfy stomach hunger we need to feed the stomach just enough food, let it do its work, and then let it rest. As we eat we need to pause periodically to check in with the stomach to discern when it is becoming comfortably full.

Cellular Hunger

When we were infants, we were tuned in to the signals from our body that told us when to eat and when to stop. Given a choice, we had an instinctive awareness of what foods and how much food our body needed. As we grew older this inner wisdom became lost in a bewildering host of other inner and outer voices that told us how we should eat. We received conflicting messages from our parents, from our peers, from advertising and health classes, from scientific research and diet doctors, and from movies and mirrors. These messages created a confusion of desires, impulses, and aversions that have rendered us unable to just eat and to eat just enough. If we are to return to a healthy and balanced relationship with food, it is essential that we learn to turn our awareness inward and to hear again what our body is always telling us about its needs and its satisfaction. To learn to listen to cellular hunger is the primary skill of mindful eating.

One of the most striking examples of cellular hunger was taught to me by a baby. I was a nervous pediatric intern on my first assignment, the emergency room at University Hospital in San Diego. On a hot summer night a young couple arrived with their one-year-old child. They had been driving several hours in one-hundred-degree heat across the desert in a car without air conditioning, from Twenty Nine Palms, where the father was stationed. In the evening they had noticed that something was wrong with their baby. He had become weak and so floppy that he was unable to sit up. This sort of history rings many alarm bells in a young doctor's mind. It raises the specter of a number of rare and life-threatening illnesses including meningitis, polio, and botulism.

I was reassured when I examined the little boy. He was alert, smiled at me, and had neurologic exam that ruled out brain infection or paralysis. His mouth and diaper were wet, so he was not dehydrated. He just seemed to lack the energy to sit up or crawl. I asked the young parents what he had been eating and drinking. Because of the heat he'd stopped eating. His parents, worried that he might get diarrhea from contaminated water, had just given him distilled water to drink, lots of it. I suddenly realized that the baby simply might be salt depleted.

Rather than doing expensive and painful blood tests, I ran to the cafeteria and returned with a bag of potato chips. When I opened it and held them out, the little boy sat up, grabbed the chips, and began eating. His parents were amazed at this sudden resurrection! I explained that their baby had been sweating profusely in the heat, losing salt and water as they traveled. The distilled water he was gulping down had only replaced the water, not the salt. He had "heard" his cells calling out for sodium chloride (salt), and as soon as he saw it, he responded.

The body has its own wisdom and can tell us a lot about what it requires if we are able to listen. Unfortunately, as we get older we become deaf to what our bodies are telling us we need. For example, people who are working and sweating in hot weather often suffer from heat prostration due to loss of sodium and chloride. Doctors have to tell them to take salt tablets. Other people have to be careful not to eat too much salt.

A common symptom of undiagnosed diabetes is incessant thirst and frequent urination. This is a good example of how the body is able to communicate its urgent needs as it tries to keep us healthy. In diabetes, the pancreas is unable to produce enough insulin to metabolize the sugar in the bloodstream. The sugar level in the body becomes too concentrated, not a happy condition for our cells. They put out a call for more water, trying to dilute the sugar, and we drink more. The kidneys then set to work flushing out both extra water and sugar by producing more urine.

How can we learn to hear the call of our cells for certain nutrients? Our body may signal hunger through symptoms such as headaches, dizziness, irritability, a light-headed feeling, or a sudden loss of energy— "pooping out." A diabetic person has to learn the difference between the body's signaling "too much sugar, give me more insulin" versus the opposite, "my blood sugar is too low, give me sugar quickly." Not to be sensitive to these signals, or to mix them up, can be dangerous.

You would think that when a person fasts the signals from their hungry cells would become overwhelming. It's curious to me that signals of hunger such as faintness or dizziness only last a few days during fasting. After that people often say they feel very energized! Maybe the body is saying, "Thanks for stopping all the junk food. I needed a rest."

On my fiftieth birthday I had a dramatic experience with cellular hunger. I had a hysterectomy after years of unsuccessful treatments for bleeding that caused severe anemia. I went into the surgery quite anemic and lost even more blood during the operation. I emerged from the anesthesia with one overwhelming desire: barbequed spareribs! This amused my friends greatly, as I had been a vegetarian for years. My body was saying, loud and clear, "I need iron to build new red blood cells! Forget that puny spinach, I need red meat!" Urgent cellular hunger can override personal habits and preferences.

Pica is a medical disorder related to cellular hunger. People with pica (rhymes with "mica") eat nonfood substances such as soil, string, paint, or wood. One form of pica occurs among pregnant women who develop a craving for clay. In the southern states there are clay banks where poor pregnant women sometimes go to dig clay to eat. Analysis of the preferred clay shows high levels of iron. Pregnant women who are building the bodies and blood of their growing fetus have an increased need for iron. If they receive prenatal vitamins with supplemental iron, the pica disappears.

Women from the American South who have moved to northern cities and lost access to this clay, however, have been seen to substitute laundry starch, which has the consistency of clay but unfortunately contains no iron and thus does not treat anemia associated with pregnancy. Poor women often cannot afford prenatal vitamins or iron-rich foods such as eggs or meat. If they fill up with starch, they are even less likely to eat good food and get adequate iron.

Thus what began as cellular hunger for a needed nutrient, iron, becomes a mind hunger for clay-like foods. Eating clay, which swells in contact with water, may satisfy stomach hunger by stopping hunger pangs, but it does not satisfy the needs of anemic cells.

SEASONAL ASPECTS OF CELLULAR HUNGER

In the autumn you may become aware of a seasonal aspect of cellular hunger. As the temperature drops the body begins to call for more food. Until recent times, when humans began living in well-heated houses, listening to and responding to this demand was essential to our survival. We needed to add a layer of insulating fat to keep our inner organs warm. We needed more calories for the work of keeping the inner furnace going. Shivering burns extra calories. In the North you could be stuck in a cold cave until the snow melted from the entrance, with dwindling supplies of food and fuel. Eating more food in the fall, while it was still abundant, was a very intelligent habit. Now that we live in warm houses and pay teenage boys to clear our driveways, so we can drive in heated cars to the supermarket when we get a craving for double-fudge ice cream, maybe it's not so intelligent to load up on calories for the winter.

How can we overcome these old "survival scripts"? First, mindfulness helps us become aware of them. We can hear the little voice inside crying, "Feed me. I'm cold!" We might even be aware of the tension of its ancient fear of death by starvation, death by freezing. We can pause to acknowledge it and to become aware of what might suffice to comfort that voice.

If we're the teenage boy who has been shoveling the driveway for two hours in subzero weather, it might be appropriate to feed that inner voice two sandwiches, some cookies, and a big mug of hot cocoa with a marshmallow on top. If we are the middle-aged homeowner who has been watching the teenage boy through double-pane windows, we might offer that voice the comfort of a slow cup of tea. It could be soothed by a hot shower or a bowl of soup eaten in the warmth of a crackling fire. There are many ways to be kind to ourselves.

Through mindfulness we can become more sensitive to cellular hunger and learn to separate what the body actually needs from what our mind is demanding. If we stop and listen carefully and often enough, eventually we might be able to do what some animals do, taste a food and "know" it is what we need. We would eat a banana when our cells asked for more potassium; carrots when we needed beta carotene; eggs or meat when we needed protein or iron; oranges or grapefruit when our cells asked for vitamin C; chocolate when we needed magnesium; and flaxseed, purslane, or fish when our body needed omega-3 oils. We would also know the difference between hunger and thirst.

We can train ourselves to listen to what our body is saying in a very simple way. We take a small pause before eating. We turn our attention inward. We ask the body what it needs to do its work.

Becoming Mindful of Cellular Hunger

1. Sit quietly, close your eyes, and become aware of the entire body. Can you discern whether the cells of the body are hungry or satisfied?
2. If they are hungry, for what? Liquid or solid? Vegetables? Root or leafy? Fruit? Citrus or not? Salt? Starch? Protein? This is not easy to discern at first. It might be easier to be aware of the signals from the body's cells if you try this before you eat. Sit for a few minutes with your eyes closed and try to read what the body actually wants.

Halfway through a meal, stop eating, close your eyes, and try to feel if the body itself is hungry now. If so, for what? At the end of the meal, stop, close your eyes, and ask again.

Sometimes what we interpret as hunger is actually cellular thirst. Before you eat a snack, try having something to drink instead, juice or a hot beverage. Sip it slowly, with awareness of temperature and taste. Now turn your attention inward and investigate whether your hunger has changed. Has it decreased, increased, or changed the foods it is asking for?

SATISFYING CELLULAR HUNGER

The essential elements satisfy cellular hunger. These include water, salt, protein, fat, carbohydrates, minerals, vitamins, and trace elements such as iron or zinc. We busy, noisy, distracted humans are not very well attuned to the sensations in the body that signal a request for a specific nutrient. At times we get a clear request: citrus! water! tomato soup! These requests often only come through when we are ill and the body insists that we be careful about what we put into it.

Asking the Body What It Needs

Next time you are ill, ask the body what it needs. You can run through your refrigerator or your shelves in your mind's eye, holding the question, "Body, please tell me what you need." A variation of this exercise, which you can do whether you are well or ill, is on track 3 on the audio CD.

Try this at the grocery store; however, it is important not to go when you are very hungry. Walk through the aisles, looking at all the types of food, saying to the body, "Tell me what you need." Hold the question lightly and see what information you get.

Mind Hunger

Mind hunger is based upon thoughts.

"I should eat more protein."
"I deserve an ice cream cone."
"I should drink twelve glasses of water a day."
"Eggs are good for you. They have lots of protein and vitamin A."
"Eggs are bad for you. They have too much cholesterol."

Mind hunger is influenced by what we take in through eyes and ears, the words we read and hear. Thousands of cookbooks provide food for mind hunger. Thousands of diet books provide food for mind hunger.

I have watched scores of dieting fads come and go during my medical career. What was good to eat one year becomes evil a decade later. The no-citrus diet ("bad for your joints") was followed by the grapefruit diet. The pasta diet was followed by the no-carbohydrates diet. The all-the-vegetables-you-can-eat diet turned around and became the high-quality-protein-only diet.

Mind hunger is often based upon absolutes and opposites: good food versus bad food, should eat versus should not eat. When I was in medical school we were taught that animal fat was bad. We were informed of the early findings of the large Framingham Study that linked consumption of animal fat with heart disease. We all renounced butter, whole milk, cream, half-and-half, cream cheese, beef, and pork. We substituted sherbet for ice cream. Eggs were rationed, two per person per week. It became alarming and even repulsive to see these dangerous foods being shoveled into a woefully ignorant mouth.

Corn oil was considered good. Corn oil margarine was endorsed by medical groups. A few years later, however, a study showed that a diet high in oil was linked to lower rates of heart attack and stroke but higher rates of cancer. Unsaturated fats were less able to protect against free-radical damage to cells. We gratefully allowed butter back on our bread. The compromise introduced by one of my professors was "better butter," whipped up out of equal parts of butter and oil.

Coconut oil was good, then bad. Recently scientists have realized that people and animals who eat a lot of coconut have healthy hearts and maybe it's OK after all. Fat was the enemy for a long time, but under the Atkins diet, it was transformed into our best friend. Now the Atkins diet seems to be fading out of fashion.

Eggs were the villains for many years. It was hard to bake anything on the two-eggs-per-week rationing plan, and recipes appeared that used only egg whites. Then an article appeared in a medical journal describing a mentally ill man who had eaten thirty-six hard-boiled eggs a day for several years and had a normal cholesterol level. Subsequent studies suggested that eating eggs does not increase one's risk of heart disease. We gratefully made beautiful whole-egg, yellow-colored omelets again. Eggs were our friends once more.

My grandmother had diverticulitis, a painful disease of the colon thought to occur when the muscles of the colon weakened from trying to digest too much fiber in the diet. She was told to eat only pale mushy foods: applesauce, mashed potatoes, custard, creamed soups. Later studies reversed this prescription, postulating that diverticulitis results from not enough fiber in the diet!

In my early years in medicine I was swayed by the latest nutritional "truths" announced by doctors and research scientists. Over the decades I have become more skeptical as I have seen the experts reverse themselves repeatedly. I've ended up not taking any absolute statements about food too seriously, whether they come from a medical journal or from within the urging of my own mind. The Buddhist principle of the middle way emerges as a very sane way to live. It advises us not to become caught up in any extremes. In the context of eating, finding the middle way means not clinging to any food and not hating any food. Don't go overboard with anything, in either a positive or negative way. Food is food. The rest is mind games.

The journalist Michael Pollan writes,

> We've learned to choose our foods by the numbers (calories, carbs, fats, RDA's, price, whatever), relying more heavily on our reading and computational skills than upon our senses. We've lost all confidence in our sense of taste and smell, which can't detect the invisible macro- and micro-nutrients science has taught us to worry about, and which food processors have become adept at deceiving anyway. The American supermarket—chilled and stocked with hermetically sealed packages bristling with information—has effectively shut out the Nose and elevated the Eye.
>
> No wonder we have become, in the midst of our astounding abundance, the world's most anxious eaters.[6]

I would suggest that we have actually shut out the nose and elevated the mind. It is the mind that makes us anxious, not the nose or eye. The mind thinks that the body would cooperate and eat perfectly if it could keep us informed about the truth, the scientific nutritional facts. When these "facts" are revealed as impermanent, a moving target, changing as new studies are done or a new medical guru appears, it creates a condition of chronic anxiety. Like Catholics who grow up anxious because they might be sinning and not even know it, the mind is anxious because we might be ingesting something dangerous and not even know it—until a new scientific study is published. When we eat based upon the thoughts in the mind, our eating is usually based in worry. When the mind is fretting about "should eat" and "should not eat," our enjoyment of what is actually in our mouth evaporates.

There are some amusing studies showing the power the mind has over our eating habits. People can be convinced to like or dislike certain foods based upon false information. Scientists have been able to lead people to believe that in childhood they had a negative experience with a certain food. Told that a "computer analysis" indicates that they became ill after eating strawberry ice cream, some participants later indicate a belief that this episode had in fact occurred. They also say that they plan to avoid the offending flavor in the future. On the flip side, positive food memories can be planted, too. In another study people were led to believe that they loved asparagus when they first tasted it. The 40 percent of people who incorporated this belief also indicated that they intended to eat more asparagus in the future.[7]

The voices that comprise mind hunger are important to hear but should be taken with a large grain of salt. "You should start the day with a big breakfast." "You should eat six times a day." "You shouldn't eat past noon." "Sugar is poison."

The notion that we should eat scientifically and that food is medicine is uniquely American. It leads us to wait anxiously for pronouncements arising from the latest research studies, and to follow the newest fad diet, especially if it is promoted by a telegenic doctor and adopted by a movie star or two. The food and beverage industry, alert to these trends, develops new products and feeds our anxiety through their advertising.

For example, in the last decade there has been an epidemic of mind-induced thirst. The minds of most modern Americans compel them to carry around a water bottle at all times and to sip from it frequently, much like a baby bottle, no matter where they are: at a business meeting, at a concert or play, in the swimming pool. This fetish began with a medical report stating that humans should drink eight to twelve glasses of water a day. Tea and coffee did not count, as they were diuretics and depleted the body of water. Your cells were crying out for water. Fearing death by dehydration, Americans began carrying glasses of water around. Product development departments noticed and responded quickly, spawning two huge new industries: bottled water and water bottles.*

I looked at a shelf of water bottles at a retreat recently. There was water shipped from Europe, Canada, Colorado, Alaska, California, Washington, and Oregon. People now try to bring personal water bottles into the meditation hall during retreats. Apparently they are unable to endure various body sensations that they interpret as "dehydration" and cannot sit still for sixty minutes without a drink. All the liquid that goes in eventually must come out. People pop up and down to the bathroom like grasshoppers.

A few years ago a corrective report announced that people had misinterpreted the first report. Humans needed a total of sixty-four ounces of liquid a day, but they did not have to drink that amount from a glass. It actually all could come from food. And coffee and tea counted. Studies showed that these caffeinated beverages didn't deplete the body's liquids after all.

Why, in the midst of this epidemic of grown-ups toting and constantly nursing from water bottles decorated with various company logos, has no one asked how our mothers and fathers and our grandparents, and the entire human race for tens of thousands of years before, escaped mass annihilation by dehydration because high-impact polycarbonate plastic bottles filled with "spring water" hadn't been invented yet? Our

---

*The National Resources Defense Council has a comprehensive report on bottled water at www.nrdc.org/water. Many people buy bottled water because it has been marketed as being safer than tap water. Actually, however, the water we buy at the store may just *be* tap water. Consumption of soft drinks has declined in recent years as consumers have realized that these drinks may not be healthy; in search of sales, soda companies have gone into the bottled water business, sometimes marketing city tap water as "spring water." In addition, water directly from the tap may be safer than water from a bottle: research indicates that polycarbonate and other plastic containers leach hormone-like chemicals into our food and drink that can disrupt reproductive health and sexual development and may contribute to cancer.[8]

modern minds believed what putative "science" and old wives' tales in magazines told us and overrode the wisdom of our bodies.

WHEN MIND HUNGER AND BODY HUNGER DON'T AGREE

I once witnessed a poignant battle between mind and body hunger. My adopted daughter had recently arrived from Vietnam. She was painfully thin and ate everything voraciously, stuffing herself so that her belly swelled visibly, and she hoarded any leftover food. She would refuse to leave the table as long as food remained in the serving dishes or on anyone's plate. One day we served something she tasted and did not like. She tried again and again to eat the food, becoming more and more upset. Her mind was telling her to eat it even if she found it repulsive, because there might not be any more food for a long time. The memory of past scarcity was trying to override her mouth and body, which were clear about what they did not want to eat.

We do this all the time. We are very full, but the mind says, "One more won't hurt." Or, as a workshop member said, "I'm really stuffed, but . . . I could eat *that*." Brian Wansink describes one study in which amnesiac patients were told it was dinnertime, and they proceeded to eat an entire meal even though their digestive tracts were still busy processing the full meal they had eaten and forgotten only thirty minutes before. In another study people were put in a room with all the food they could eat and a clock that ran two hours fast. Overweight subjects tended to eat more frequently based upon what their mind told them about "mealtime" as they read it off the clock. Normal-weight subjects tended to eat less often, relying upon their internal cues of hunger.[9]

At our silent lunch on the first day of a mindful eating retreat, just as seconds were being passed, I announced, "Here at the monastery lunch is our largest meal of the day. Supper will be light." That afternoon many people reported that they had been feeling quite satisfied after their first helping at lunch. However, as soon as they heard my announcement their minds jumped to scarcity mode, and they found themselves taking second helpings. These were helpings that their eyes, mouth, stomach, and body did not desire! They said that they could hear their minds saying, "You better store up. Supper will be light. Maybe you'll be hungry afterward." This is a clear example of mind hunger overriding all the other signals of fullness and satisfaction.

This is exactly what lies at the heart of our current disturbed relationship to eating and food. Our minds do not always tell us the truth. In order to restore a harmonious relationship to eating, in order to enjoy our food, we must learn to listen to the deeper wisdom of our body.

EXERCISES

Becoming Aware of Mind Hunger

During the day become aware of what the mind is telling you about food and drink. Listen for the mind's comments on what you "should" eat or "should" drink and "should not" eat or drink. Notice whether there are competing voices that say different things about the same food. For example, the mind might be saying, "I'm really thirsty. I'd like a Coke." Another voice says, "Coke is bad for you. Don't you remember, you can dissolve a tooth in Coke? Get juice instead." Another voice says, "You need the caffeine. You're falling asleep at the wheel. Get a Coke." Yet another voice says, "You're addicted to caffeine. You should be able to stay awake without it. Start your caffeine fast right now."

Before you eat, pause and look at the food. Listen inwardly to hear what the mind is saying about this food and drink before you.

What is the mind is saying about hunger? Is hunger "good" or "bad"? Check the eyes, stomach, body, and mind to see where hunger might lie.

What is the mind is saying about satisfaction? Check before, during, and after the meal. Move the mind's awareness to the mouth, the stomach, and the body. What parts are satisfied? What parts are not?

As you read articles about scientific studies of food, become aware of any "shoulds" or "should nots" that are forming in the mind. Remember that this scientific information changes frequently. If you are using this book in a class, you can bring some articles to class that illustrate the American "scientific" or "medical" approach to eating. It's especially interesting to point out the contradictions and reversals that emerge, such as the recommendation not to eat coconut oil and then the news that coconut oil may be good for you.

SATISFYING MIND HUNGER

I'm not sure we can ever really satisfy mind hunger, because the mind is always changing its mind. One day it puts us on a strict diet, the next day it convinces us we need another dessert. The mind also contains the inner critic, a voice that criticizes us no matter what we eat or drink (more on this voice in chapter 4).

Please investigate this for yourself. What satisfies mind hunger?

Often the mind feeds on information, on news, on gossip. The mind likes to learn new things, to digest new information. Let's say that you are eating at a fast-food place. On the table is a place mat with nutritional information on the foods you are eating. As you eat a cheeseburger, your mind is taking in the nutritional content of your cheeseburger. The mind might be satisfied to learn that this restaurant has switched to cooking without trans fats. This is interesting information, but is it truly satisfying? No. Why not? Because this type of information, what is "good" or "bad" to eat, is always changing. Forty years ago, trans fat–laden margarine was good, and Crisco and lard were staples in our diet. The mind knows that knowledge is always changing, so it can never be at ease.

The mind is truly content only when it becomes quiet. When the many and contradictory voices around eating are still, when the awareness function is dominant over the thinking function, then we can be fully present as we eat. When we are filled with awareness, we become filled with satisfaction.

Heart Hunger

I became aware of heart hunger through the comments of participants in our mindful eating workshops. They talked longingly of foods they had eaten for family holidays, foods their mother had made for them when they were ill, foods eaten with people they loved. It was clear that the particular foods were not as important as the mood or emotion they evoked. Hunger for these foods arose from the desire to be loved and cared for. The memory of those special times infused these foods with warmth and happiness.

One woman said that the mindful way we ate in the monastery had suddenly evoked memories of eating with her grandparents. She and her siblings had spent childhood summers at their grandparents' farm. There, meals were slow affairs, with grace before eating and intervals of silence to appreciate the food, which was homegrown, home preserved, and home cooked. She remembered,

> Grandma had a "feel" for making bread. We'd compare crusts and tastes like some people savor a fine wine. She told me that making bread was like taking care of a baby, "You don't want to get it in a draft." Grandfather had Bells' palsy and chewed quite slowly and carefully. He would finish twenty minutes after everyone else. We all sat at the table and waited for him, though not in silence. He would compare the virtues of the several varieties of corn and tomatoes on the table, urging the children to really taste them! Grandmother would talk about what she had canned when, peaches, plums, pickles, jams. I would leave from a visit with them feeling very "full." They had a way of being present to me although I can't say we had any earth-shattering talks.

No, not earth-shattering, but heart-nourishing. It was food grown with love, shared and eaten in love. Her grandparents had taught her about mindful eating, but she had forgotten their lessons until she came to the retreat and slowed down, eating again with awareness and appreciation. After the workshop she wrote me, "Sometimes I have felt deprivation around eating. I realize now it was only my perception. I actually was in the midst of abundance and richness. I lacked the mindfulness to appreciate the food at hand."

Many people are aware that they eat in an attempt to fill a hole, not in the stomach but in the heart. We eat when we are lonely. We eat when a relationship ends. We eat when someone dies, taking food to the home of those who are grieving. These are the ways we try to take care of ourselves and others, but we must understand that food put into the stomach will never ease the emptiness, the ache in a heart.

Curt came to mindful eating classes with a history of dieting since he was a teenager. He was a veteran of hundreds of diets and many years in Overeaters Anonymous. He had been fairly skeptical about the utility of mindful eating until we did an exercise in the next-to-last class. We passed around a plate of thinly sliced apples arranged on a bed of fern leaves with pink azalea flowers. Everyone took in the color, form and texture of the apples with their eyes, took in their fragrance with deep inhalations, and then slowly ate one slice. When it was his turn to relate his experience, I was ready for a bitter comment about how for him a whole apple was one bite and a whole apple pie was one serving.

Instead his face softened and his eyes filled with tears. He looked like a little boy.

He said in wonder, "I was transported back to my grandmother's home. She had built a house in an old apple orchard. The trees still bore apples, large ones, and we always ate them when we went to visit her. When I tasted this little slice of apple I was right there, back in her kitchen! I could smell it and see it, right down to the pattern on the linoleum on the floor."

"You have just fed the heart's hunger," I said.

Later Curt told me that his comfort foods were slow-baked beans, split pea soup, and "anything cooked from scratch out of the Fanny Farmer cookbook." Why?

Because it meant that Momma wasn't drinking. When she was sober she'd pull out that book and cook for us kids, things that took hours to prepare. It was the only time she was really present and showed that she loved us. Just the sight of that cookbook made me feel good. I've searched used bookstores for that particular edition but haven't ever found it.

It's no mystery that many comfort foods are the things our mother or grandmother made us when we were sick, or the foods we ate with the family on holidays. For each person the food that is flavored with love is different. It could be chicken soup, custard, mashed potatoes, or cinnamon toast.

When I was six years old I had a lingering, mysterious illness, with fever and swollen glands, enough like leukemia to scare everyone including our family doctor. I had to be taken into the city for blood tests. Each time I cried, but sat unmoving in the face of what seemed like an enormous needle. The reward was an ice cream cone. Ice cream at that time was an uncommon treat. We were not poor, but not rich, and had to drive ten miles to an ice cream store that had only four flavors of ice cream: vanilla, chocolate, strawberry, and the flavor of the week.

Now my parents are dead, and I can buy at least sixty kinds of ice cream in any supermarket, but I seldom keep ice cream at home. It would lose its power. It is my own reward, my own way of caring for myself. If I undergo an ordeal, such as a particularly hard day or week at work, when I emerge, I reward myself with ice cream. I take myself out to an ice cream shop, take my time choosing a flavor, and savor every lick. It is a ritual that feeds the hunger of my heart. I am honoring the kindness of my parents and my earnest wish that every child could be so lovingly nourished.

We feed our heart when we take care in preparing food for ourselves, treating ourselves as well as we would a guest. It only takes a few minutes to arrange food nicely on a plate rather than eating out of a cardboard take-home carton, or to sit down at a table you have set with a colorful place mat and candle rather than eating standing up at the kitchen counter.

A few years ago I ate dinner in a restaurant with an old friend who was critical of the food we had been served. He told me that he was always searching for the perfect meal. He could remember a few exceptional meals in his lifetime. When he described them it was clear that it was not the memory of the perfect entrée or dessert wine that had created this longing. It was the food for the heart, the all-too-brief experience of interconnectedness with his dinner companions, that he longed to find again.

During the mindful eating workshops, as we try different exercises, people often have memories suddenly float to the surface of consciousness. Once, as we were sharing our lists of comfort foods, one woman read out, "Raspberry yogurt." She began to say, "I don't know why I like only raspberry flavor—" and suddenly she exclaimed, "Oh! I just remembered that my grandmother loved raspberry jam. She was a diabetic, and wasn't supposed to have it, but she had some jam hidden that she would share with me when I was a little girl. It was our special secret."

When you talk with people at any length about comfort foods, you will always uncover a story that is warm with feelings of connection, love, and companionship. All the rich food in the world will not fill our heart's hunger. The heart is nourished by intimacy with others.

There are remarkable stories about people in concentration camps who, in the midst of torture, death, and deliberate starvation by their captors, still found ways to feed the heart's hunger. Some women in German concentration camps, for instance, shared their favorite family recipes, creating oral cookbooks. Teaching each other, memorizing another woman's recipes, they created friendship, hope, and an optimism that some aspect of their lives might survive the camp and nourish others.[10]

During World War II a group of women prisoners in a Japanese concentration camp in Sumatra wrote down musical scores from memory and formed a choir. Too weak to stand, they performed sitting down.

Half the choir died in a year's time. But they forgot the terrible hunger of their emaciated bodies as their hearts were filled with the music they created together. "Each time [we had a concert] again it seemed a miracle, that among those cockroaches and rats, and the bedbugs and the dysentery, the smells of the latrines, that there could be that much beauty, that women's voices could actually do this, and bring this to this horrid camp," one of the singers later recalled.[11]

We cannot always depend upon others to fulfill our desire for intimacy, however, because people are always changing. They move away, they fall out of love with us and into love with someone else, they get Alzheimer's and think we are a stranger, and eventually they die.

A woman at a workshop choked up as she told of being in a puzzling transition. She was an excellent cook and for many years she had taken great pride in feeding her husband and three boys home-cooked meals. Now her sons were grown. The last time they had come home, they said, "Mom, you are always so busy feeding us that you never sit down with us at the table. Come sit down." She couldn't understand why they weren't interested in her food anymore. I told her, "When they were boys, you fed their stomachs and, at the same time, their hearts, because you cooked with love. Now they are men who can buy whatever they wish to feed the hunger of their stomachs. Now they know that life passes quickly and that time together is precious. They are asking that you sit down and be present with them, talk, tell stories, and laugh with them. They are asking for time with you, time that will nourish the hunger of their hearts."

We cannot depend upon food to fill the empty place in our heart. Ultimately what must nourish our heart is intimacy with this very moment. We can experience this intimacy with anything that presents itself to us, people or plants, rocks, rice, or raisins. This is what being present brings us to, the sweet and poignant taste of true presence. When this presence fills us, all hungers vanish. All things, just as they are, are perfect satisfaction.

Becoming Aware of Heart Hunger

What foods do you eat when you are sad or lonely? Make a list. If you are working in a mindful eating group, read these lists to each other.

When, between meals, you feel the impulse to have a snack or a drink, please look at what you were feeling just *before* that impulse arose.

If you have the snack or drink, does anything change?

When you become aware of heart hunger, pick a favorite comfort food. Buy a small portion or single helping, such as one special chocolate truffle or a single scoop of good ice cream. Sit down and look at the food with love. Eat it very slowly. As you swallow each bite, imagine sending it to your heart (before your stomach and body), infused with grandmotherly kindness and love. (If your grandmother was a bear, pick someone you know who is kind.)

EATING TO CHANGE YOUR HEART

At our monastery, when we ask people to notice what they were feeling right before they felt the urge to snack, people discover an array of emotions that have occurred. They include frustration, sadness, irritation, boredom, anxiety, disappointment, anger, confusion, insecurity, and impatience. Notice that these emotions all fall into the category of negative or aversive feelings.

This finding raises some interesting questions. Do we often eat in order to change the state of our mind and heart? Do we eat to rid ourselves of uncomfortable feelings?

Many people in the workshops on mindful eating tell us that they feel a huge hole in their heart. They might relate it to the death of a loved person or animal. It might be experienced as sadness, or as loneliness, or as the feeling of not quite belonging or fitting anywhere. The First

Noble Truth of Buddhism is that to live as a human being is to experience suffering. For most of us it is not the suffering of being caught in war or tortured. It is more subtle. As a teenaged girl told me sadly, "I always feel like something is wrong, but I don't know what it is. And I don't know how to fix it." There is an underlying, pervasive, restless feeling of unsatisfactoriness. There is a gap between you and the rest of the world. You eat, but you don't really taste or enjoy.

Most unbalanced relationships with food are caused by being unaware of heart hunger. No food can ever satisfy this form of hunger. To satisfy it, we must learn how to nourish our hearts. We will not find full satisfaction in food, no matter how delicious, if we do not nourish the heart on a daily basis. Conversely, when we are mindful with eating, a feeling of intimacy and connection will arise. Then any food can nourish the heart.

SATISFYING HEART HUNGER

Heart hunger is satisfied by intimacy. Each of us is fundamentally alone in the world. No one can know us to the bottom of our being. No one can know all our thoughts. No one can know completely the deepest longings of our hearts. No one, not even the person we are closest to, can experience life as we do.

The realization that we are fundamentally alone can be a source of sadness, of grief. More dangerously, it can lead us to try unhealthy ways to create a false sense of intimacy, such as abusing drugs, sex, or food. Many people hang out in bars, waiting in vain for their "soul mate" to wander in. They settle for a series of brief and disappointing sexual encounters. Many people try to solve their loneliness by maintaining Internet relationships, relationships that are essentially based upon fantasy.

Eating can be another way to relieve loneliness. As long as I am busy with an all-important activity like eating, I am distracted from my plight, my situation as an individual living in isolation, separated forever from all of the "others" in the universe.

Most people feel self-conscious about eating alone. There is an awkwardness about eating alone in a restaurant. It seems to imply that you have no friends. If they are eating alone at home most people will turn on the TV, a way of creating the illusion of intimacy, the feeling that their house is filled with people and activity.

By contrast, people who are practicing mindful eating deliberately create times and search out places to eat alone. They are relieved to be doing one thing at a time, simply eating, sheltered from the distractions of talking, reading, or watching TV.

When we eat and look deeply into our food, we are in the company of many beings: the plants, animals, and people whose life energy was poured into the food on our plate. According to the Zen teachings, each time we eat, we take in the life energy of countless beings into our bodies. The food on our plate is the product of the sun, the earth, the rain, the insects who pollinate the plants, and many people, including farmers, truck drivers, and grocers. This energy, which is the product of so many beings, courses through our body, propelled by every beat of our heart. It travels to the farthest cells, to our toenails and to the tips of our hair. These beings literally become us, our blue or brown eyes, our soft lips, our hard white teeth, our loving heart. This daily miracle of transubstantiation occurs in our own bodies, day and night.

Unfortunately, while this miracle is occurring we are mostly unaware of it. To awaken to it, even for a few moments each day, can give us new joy, no matter how difficult the other circumstances of our life may be. It can give us new energy, no matter what our age or how tired we are. If we eat with our mind open and aware we can experience our intimate connection to these many beings, and our loneliness dissolves.

EXERCISE

Satisfying Heart Hunger

When you feel hungry, but a check of the seven hungers reveals that the mouth, stomach, and body are not hungry, do something deliberate to nourish the heart. Here are some ideas. Talk to a person you love, play with a child or a pet, work in your garden, create something, listen to your favorite music, give a gift. If you eat, eat slowly, and open your awareness to the multitude of beings who brought this food to your table. Give thanks.

Putting It All Together

Now you are becoming aware of the seven hungers. Three of the seven tend to be more problematic in our lives than the others. They are mouth hunger, heart hunger, and mind hunger. These forms of hunger often cause us to overeat—but only when we remain unaware of them and of how to go about satisfying them.

Now that you've explored the seven types of hunger, you can develop an essential skill of mindful eating: assessing the level of each kind of hunger whenever the desire to eat arises. In order to know which kind of hunger we are feeling, we can make it a regular practice to ask the question, "Who in there is hungry?"

To find this out, we have to pause before we eat. At first assessing the seven hungers may be difficult, but once you learn this skill, it will take only a few seconds, and you will be able to do it in the company of others without their noticing. Even if they do notice and ask what you are doing, you can say, "I'm checking in with my body to see which parts are hungry and what they are asking for." With some people you will be able to add, "I'm practicing mindful eating." This might be the start of an interesting conversation.

EXERCISE

Who Is Hungry in There?

This is the most important exercise in this book. It is the essence of mindful eating. Please do it at every meal, until it becomes second nature. This exercise is also included on the audio CD, on track 4.

Each of the seven hungers is associated with a different part of the body. Before eating or drinking, look inward and ask each of these parts if it is hungry. If the answer is yes, ask that part how hungry it is on a scale of zero (not interested at all) to ten (famished).

To review: the parts of the body we look to are the eyes, nose, mouth, stomach, cells, mind, and heart.

Example: You see some donuts at work. The eyes might say, "They were left over from yesterday's party, but they look OK. Maybe we should have one." *Eye hunger registers a three on the hunger scale.*

The nose might say, "I can't help out. I can't smell anything. If I can't smell them, I'm not interested in them at all." *Zero nose hunger.*

The mouth says, "Any sensation is better than an empty mouth. Let's try them." *Mouth hunger is a five.*

The stomach says, "After all that coffee you drank in the car I feel a little shaky and slightly nauseated. I'm not interested in taking in anything right now." *Stomach hunger is zero.*

The cells say, "Stale fat and sugar? Not good for any of our cells." *Cellular hunger is also a zero.*

The mind says, "Well, we really shouldn't eat a donut because we're trying to eat in a more healthy way. You did well this morning, with only a glass of orange juice and a half cup of yogurt for breakfast. You didn't have any carbs though . . . maybe you could have half a donut at coffee break, if you work hard all morning." Then the mind continues, "On the other hand, those donuts might be gone by coffee break, so maybe we better get one now. You could take one and break it in half. We'll do some isometric exercises in our cubicle to make up for it." *Mind hunger is a six.*

The heart says, "I'm dreading starting this new project. I just can't seem to wrap my mind around it. I have no idea where to start. My mother always said that you work better with a good breakfast. I don't think we had a good breakfast. Sugar soothes me and a donut could help me think better. I saw Susan in the lunchroom. She's easy to talk to. Let's go get a donut and talk with her for a while." *The heart registers hunger at eight.*

In this example, the hunger of mind and heart override the messages from the poor stomach and cells, who aren't hungry at all. This is very common. People eat not because their body needs food, but because they are anxious or sad, or because the clock says it's 12 P.M., or because "everyone else is eating," or because "it would be a waste of good food to throw it away," or because "there might not be any left later."

Once you learn to investigate who inside you is hungry, and make it a regular routine to stop and do this exercise before you eat, then you can make a more informed decision about whether to eat or not. Only food or drink will satisfy stomach and cellular hunger; however, there are many alternatives to food for satisfying the other five types of hunger.

If we want to feel satisfied and eat the appropriate amount, we have to take food in through all the sense doors, becoming awake to the color, fragrance, texture, taste, temperature, and sound of our food. And if we want to be content in this moment and to be nourished by whatever comes into our life, we also must find ways to feed our heart.

3 | Exploring Our Habits and Patterns with Food

IN THE LAST CHAPTER we explored one of the essential skills of mindful eating: bringing our full awareness and attention to hunger itself so that we can know what exactly we're hungry for and how to satisfy it. Another important aspect of mindful eating is becoming more aware of the eating habits and patterns we've developed throughout our lives—what is often called our conditioning.

When we read the word "conditioning" we might think of Pavlov's experiments with dogs. As the dogs were fed, a bell was rung. After some time the dogs would salivate whenever they heard the sound of the bell, even when no food appeared. Their cells in their bodies and brains reacted to the sound alone.

Humans also form connections like this. When we receive positive rewards, like praise, smiles, kisses, or pleasurable sensations from food, we are more likely to continue a behavior. When we receive negative feedback, scolding, frowns, rejection, or unpleasant sensations such as a swat on the behind, we are less likely to continue a behavior. Food itself is intrinsically neither good nor bad. We learn "good food" or "bad food" through experience. A crawling baby may put anything he finds on the ground, including dead animals or worms, into his mouth and chew happily until his mother shrieks, "Ugh, that's dirty. Bad boy!" She jabs her finger into his mouth to dig out his tasty morsel and eventually teaches (conditions) him to wash his hands, sit at a table, and eat proper food with a fork and knife. However, if this baby were raised in the wild by dogs or wolves, he would prefer raw meat eaten right off the ground.

Although our food choices are affected by social conditioning, some foods such as sugar, salt, and fat provide their own positive reinforcement in the form of pleasant taste sensations and a lift in our mood. Other potential foods provide the opposite. One episode of vomiting after eating rhubarb leaves or blisters in the mouth from snacking on poison ivy provides pretty potent negative conditioning. Positive conditioning results in desire; negative conditioning results in aversion.

Conditioning is a normal, unavoidable phenomenon in all our lives. Conditioning around food begins as soon as we are born. As we drink warm milk we are being cuddled by our mother, skin on warm skin. Breast milk is surprisingly sweet. It is not a surprise, then, that when people make a list of comfort foods, many of these foods are white, milky, creamy, rich, or sweet, such as ice cream, macaroni and cheese, mashed potatoes with butter, a bowl of creamed soup, a latte with whipped cream, hot cocoa, or even a basic glass of warm milk.

When we cry, we are comforted by being picked up and given a nipple to suck on. Researchers can assess a baby's distress by measuring their sucking rate. The more distressed, the more sucks per minute. Rags or pacifiers dipped in sugar have been used for generations to quiet babies. Pacifiers, or "binkies," are now sold by the millions based upon the comfort provided by sucking. They are even used to decrease babies' crying during circumcision. It is not a surprise, then, to see how popular personal water bottles and flavored waters have become of late. It is a legitimate way for an adult to relieve stress by "nursing" throughout the day. A more subtle form of comfort is the never-empty cup of warm coffee or tea carried about throughout the workday. Our minds and bodies have formed this link: stress + warm drink = comfort (lessening of stress)

As we grow the conditioning continues. The conditioning can be positive or negative. We will form very different associations and habit patterns when we eat something and our mother beams and says, "Good boy! You ate it all up!" versus her frowning and saying, "Don't be such a pig!" A little girl who is warned, "If you eat too much you'll get fat like your mom!" is being directed on a very different path from a boy who is praised with, "What a great appetite he has! He's going to grow up to be bigger than his daddy!"

In research on how couples eat on a date, women report that to "overeat" on a date would not be feminine, while men feel that overeating is a sign of being manly or powerful. In one experiment, men read a long and detailed description of a man named Brad going out on a date. There were two versions of the story, that differed only in these few words. Brad either ate "most" of his popcorn or "a few handfuls" of his popcorn. Young men who read the "most" version rated Brad as stronger, more aggressive, more masculine, and able to bench-press more weight. Interestingly, women were not affected either positively or negatively by the few words characterizing Brad as having a big or small appetite.[1]

Our relationship to food is conditioned by thousands of influences: our family of origin, advertising, television, movies, books, magazines, our peer groups, our culture. Have you noticed that if you read about a certain food in a book, or see it in a movie, you begin to be hungry for it? A few years ago there was a popular series of books about a minister in a fictional small town in North Carolina. One of the characters, a lady named Esther, had a secret recipe for an orange marmalade cake that always sold out at annual church bazaars. So many readers developed a craving for a cake that they had never tasted, but only read about, that the author wrote a small book featuring the recipe. I even baked this cake, but I was disappointed to find that it didn't taste as delicious as the (imaginary) cake described by the (imaginary) people in the book.

If you were raised in a difficult family, mealtimes may have been very unpleasant. Perhaps they were always disharmonious or tense occasions, when anger could erupt suddenly, for no clear reason. Perhaps it was the time when all your misdeeds, real or imagined, were named and publicly criticized. Maybe you were told that you were stupid or worthless or had ruined your parent's life. Maybe you were ridiculed, called clumsy or fat or more humiliating names. You wanted to run, but if you had left the table, the verbal and emotional abuse would have escalated.

In Pavlov's experiments with dogs, food was paired with a bell.

Perhaps in your home, food was paired with stress, shame, anxiety, and danger. In Pavlov's experiments, the sound of a bell made the conditioned dogs salivate. Because human beings are more complex than dogs, and because our environment is not as simple and controlled as a cage in a laboratory, there could be many different results, many possible behaviors, that result from the pairing of eating with stress.

Even after you grew up, left home, and could eat alone in safety, events could trigger the body and mind to react as they did when you were a child. Because feeling hungry meant having to enter a place of peril in your childhood, as an adult you might react to feelings of hunger as if they were dangerous. You might try to prevent these "dangerous" sensations of hunger from arising by continuously "grazing" or by sipping sodas. You might confuse the sensations of anxiety and hunger, eating to relieve "hunger pangs" that actually are gastrointestinal signals of emotional distress.

Because the family table was the scene of unhappiness, you may feel subtle anxiety when you sit down at a table to eat. Thus you prefer to eat standing up at the refrigerator or in the kitchen. Maybe it helps to be distracted, so you eat while watching TV or in your car. Perhaps you only feel safe eating in restaurants because your family never acted out in a public place.

Let's say that your family had its difficulties, but at Thanksgiving time everyone gathered at Grandma's house and all bickering and arguments ceased. Tension dissolved like butter melting on mashed potatoes. Harmony prevailed as everyone joined in the pleasure of eating and reminiscing about the good old days. Now, as an adult, every time you have an argument with a family member, or when the "family" of internal voices in your mind are arguing and being critical of you, you may find yourself overeating on purpose, to the point where you are too stuffed to think and the voices are temporarily silent.

This is called "self-soothing." It is a way of using food to help disguise or dispel uncomfortable feelings and inner voices. They won't stay silent for long, however. As soon as you wake from your food-induced lethargy they will have fresh fuel for self-criticism.

These "eat fast and run" or "snack continuously to avoid hunger" or "eat into a stupor" behaviors were good strategies when you were a child and doing the best you could in an inescapable and repeatedly abusive situation. However, using food this way is not a healthy and happy way to eat when you are an adult.

Will it make you eat more or less if stress and eating were paired in early life? It depends. The old linkage of anxiety with eating could make you lose your appetite and eat less. The sight or taste of certain foods that you had as a child could make your body react with a faster heart rate, nausea, and secretion of hormones related to stress. Let's imagine that you come home late from a long, tense meeting at work and your spouse or partner has to reheat a homemade dinner that has now grown cold. Your stomach is in knots before the meal arrives, and you just can't eat it. Your spouse then feels disappointed and hurt. Your insides continue to register the disharmony in the air, anxiety combined with pangs of hunger, and you go to bed early with a stomachache.

However, the old pairing of anxiety with eating could have the opposite effect. It could make you eat more, especially more of comfort foods. Perhaps you come home unhappy about the outcome of a week of hard work and you overeat to the point of numbness and then watch a funny movie on TV. The show is about a man who is fired from his job and ends up living with the homeless under a bridge. It doesn't seem so funny to you. In fact, you are feeling anxious again, so you rummage around in the refrigerator, finding an open half gallon of mocha fudge ice cream that you eat surreptitiously while standing over the sink. In the bathroom mirror, as you take your anticholesterol pill, you see a smudge of chocolate around your mouth and become aware of how much fat you have just consumed. You get into bed with your spouse, feeling simultaneously guilty and defensive.

You can see how the soup of old conditioning, operating at the subconscious level, can be stirred round with new ingredients in our life to create a bitter stew of ongoing suffering.

A common form of conditioning occurs when children are told, "Clean your plate!" This is particularly potent if we are made to feel guilty about malnourished children on the other side of the globe. This instruction tells us to ignore signals from our stomach and to rely instead on the signal of an empty plate to decide when we've had "enough." Research shows that this is exactly how most people in North America decide when to stop eating. When asked how they decide when to stop eating, only 20 percent of people say they decide based upon clues from their body, such as when they feel full or no longer hungry. The rest depend upon visual cues, such as when a bowl is half or completely empty. They stop when the plate or bowl, regardless of size, is empty. As we saw in chapter 2, even if a soup bowl is rigged so that it will never empty, people will keep on eating until they're told to stop.

Many people who come to our mindful eating workshops do not know how to tell when their body is satisfied with the amount they have eaten. The only signals they are able to recognize are "uncomfortable-hungry" and "uncomfortable-stuffed-full." When they eat, they bypass the more subtle signal of "satisfied" and eat until they feel discomfort from being overly full. They consistently overeat and thus gain weight, particularly if they are eating calorie-dense foods. Bariatric surgery works in part by exaggerating the signals from the gastrointestinal tract so that patients cannot ignore them. If they do, and try to eat sugar, fat, or more than a small amount of food, they will suffer abdominal pain, nausea, vomiting, faintness, and diarrhea.

Why did our grandparents or parents give us (the potentially lethal) instruction to clean our plates? They may have been reacting to memories of hunger they felt when they were poor, or during the war or the Great Depression. Perhaps they resolved then that their children would never go hungry. Their nagging is actually a sign of their love, but it doesn't feel like love to their children. It makes them feel criticized, guilty, and confused. If there are babies starving in Africa, which is worse: to eat or not eat the large steak on your plate?

This nagging about food can also create rebellious children. I once knew an intelligent university professor and his intelligent wife who enforced the clean-your-plate-or-else rule. Their doubly intelligent kids would meekly obey so they could be excused quickly to run outside and play. They became the neighborhood's champion vomiters. This was probably not the outcome the parents intended.

Hints for Identifying Conditioned Behaviors

Most of the habit patterns we create in childhood are harmless and fade away. Ideally, as we mature we become more flexible and are able to recognize conditioned patterns of behavior and free ourselves from them. Many reactive patterns, however, are deeply held. They remain hidden and constrain us. How can we detect that an old conditioned habit pattern has been activated? There are several clues. They are idiosyncratic eating, anger, overwhelming desire, and going unconscious.

IDIOSYNCRATIC EATING

In reaction to various events in childhood, everyone develops idiosyncratic habits around eating. Research confirms the power of conditioning, for instance, on the order in which people eat foods. People who were the youngest or from a large family tend to eat a favorite food first. They learned in childhood not to wait to eat a food they liked. It might be grabbed and gone before they knew what happened. People who were only children or the oldest are more relaxed and tend to leave a favorite food to eat last.[2]

My mother was an only child, but she always ate the icing off her cake first. She did this because as a child she once set the icing aside to eat last. She was dismayed when my grandmother speared it with a fork and popped it into her mouth, saying, "Oh, if you don't want to eat this, I will." The incensed little girl resolved never to be cheated of her icing again. My mother was conscious of this habit pattern and how it arose. She could laugh about it. She was able to be flexible and eat her icing last without feeling distressed. Most of our conditioned habits, however, remain unconscious and therefore hidden to us unless someone points them out to us.

A man who attended a mindful eating workshop had stunned his family when he abruptly got up during a tense discussion about serious health issues and sped away to get ice cream and root beer "that nobody needed or wanted." When questioned about this odd behavior he recalled, "When I was growing up we rarely had desserts. But once in a while my dad, who never cooked, would make us root beer floats. It was a huge treat. Even looking at a bottle of Dad's Root Beer brings back those memories and makes me happy. I realize that when I ran out to buy ice cream and root beer I was thinking, 'I'm going to fix this. Everything's going to be wonderful. I'll make everyone happy again.'"

Sometimes we must rely on others' observations to see in what ways our eating might be idiosyncratic. My father once commented, "Oh, I see you still eat the same way you did when you were a child. You always ate only one thing at a time." I wasn't consciously aware of this habit pattern, but when I watched myself eat, he was right. I remembered that as a child I didn't like foods to touch. I liked to keep them separate on my plate, so beet juice wouldn't "bleed" into the peas or the applesauce. I didn't even like to mix tastes and would eat all of one kind of food on the plate before beginning on another. I would rotate a glass of milk so as not to drink from a place on the rim I had already used. Only when I became aware of this pattern could I sense the old childish anxiety that lay beneath it and enter the freedom that came with letting it go.

ANGER

At the Zen monastery where I live and teach, food is passed down the table and held at a side table while we chant and eat first portions in silence. Then the food is passed back up to the top so that everyone has the option of taking seconds. During the mindful eating workshops some people noticed that anger arose when seconds were being passed. I can often predict who these people will be, because they can't help looking down the table to see what kind and amount of food is coming, and how much others are taking.

In a discussion after the meal, a workshop participant said that she really liked the lasagna and was hoping for a second helping, but when the pan reached her, it was all gone and she felt upset. She told us,

> The funny thing is, my stomach was completely satisfied with the amount of lasagna I had eaten already, but my mind wanted more. Then I remembered the feeling I had when I was a child. I was the youngest of five kids. My big brothers would always grab the food as soon as it hit the table, and I had to be quick if I wanted to eat at all. I realized that when I'm eating with others I'm always watching to see that people don't take more than their "fair share."

Concentration camp survivors report becoming quite distressed if they have to stand in line for food or if they see food being thrown away, even when it has spoiled; likewise, they say that they often become anxious when food is not readily available.[3]

OVERWHELMING DESIRE

One Friday night as I was driving home from work I realized that I was out of balance with a particular food. It had been a hard week, with way too much suffering coming in the door of our child abuse program. I had been looking forward to a relaxing weekend at home when an emergency rape case came in, half an hour before closing time. You cannot rush these cases, especially when you are collecting evidence. By the time we finished it was eight o'clock. I was driving home on the freeway and found my mind searching the car for . . . chocolate! Was there any in my purse? Nope, ate that yesterday. My mind turned to the glove compartment. A one-handed search turned up nothing, as did a rummage through both map pockets and a grope through the dust balls under the seats. Should I stop at a convenience store for a fix of inferior milk chocolate or wait until I got home for a spoonful of the emergency jar of Nutella hidden at the back of the pantry shelf?

My mind was in the grip of an overwhelming desire for one food, chocolate. Almost everyone laughs when I tell this story. It is laughter of recognition. They then reveal that they also have an "addiction" to some kind of food. They recognize that this food "calls" to them when they are upset and that they eat more of it than they "should." Often they eat it faster than usual and afterward they feel uncomfortably full, guilty, or ashamed.

GOING UNCONSCIOUS

While it is common to overeat once in a while, especially at holidays or festivals, people with binge-eating disorder succumb to eating episodes that are out of their control every few days, consuming thousands of calories in an hour or two. They may be aware that their goal is to go unconscious, to briefly forget painful emotions, fear, loneliness, and the feeling that they are failing. Sometimes we eat to go unconscious and sometimes we go unconscious while eating. Both can point to hidden habit patterns involving food.

When I was an intern working forty-eight-hour shifts, I would go down to the X-ray department at night, lie on the warm developing machine and eat a frozen Ding Dong. I don't even like Ding Dongs, but the cold, creamy sugar and warm metal helped numb my physical and mental stress so I could continue to work with others in worse distress.

The point of mindful eating is not to forbid ourselves to ever use food in this way. The point is that by eating with mindfulness we can become aware of the seductive power of the call to go unconscious. As we become aware, we are creating a larger frame around what is happening in our body-mind complex. This larger space gives us flexibility, the freedom to live life on purpose. With each conscious choice, whether we ultimately choose a Ding Dong or a protein shake, a greater degree of sanity enters our life.

The Power of Awareness

How can we work with unconscious conditioning in order to unwind ourselves from its painful embrace? Awareness is the key. Our desire to be awake, to see clearly how our blind spots make us and others suffer, has to be stronger than our desire to live on automatic pilot. It's not a simple, once-made-always-kept decision. It's a decision we will face again and again.

Most of the time we talk about anger as a destructive emotion, one that we work to dissolve. But anger can be a powerful teacher. It is a call to wake up, a signal that an unconscious pattern has been activated, that our illusions, our invisible protective ego defense shields, have been poked. Once they have been poked, they are no longer invisible. We can begin to see what they are and work with loosening them. For example, if someone serves me a plate of food with beet juice running into the salad and coloring the mashed potatoes, I might find myself thinking indignantly, "She's not a very neat person."

If I am aware of my mind, I can detect that there is something extra going on. I can feel the extra "heat" of this internal judgment. I can hear the mind developing a confirmatory story. "Yes," my mind says to itself, "I noticed the trash in her bathroom hadn't been emptied before we arrived." My mind begins to rummage through its closet of old grievances. If I can stop the stories and return to the reality of a plate of food in my hands, the weight, the aromas, the colors, the shapes, then I can enjoy eating the food and feel gratitude for the one who prepared it and served it to me.

I can see again that suffering originates with me. "Oh, this is just a plate of colors and shapes. It is a gift. It has activated my old anxiety about foods not touching. I can see that rutted mind-path and I will not go down it tonight. I will stay with what is, here, now."

How can we break old habit patterns? The answer is deceptively simple but not so easy to carry out. We break old habits by being aware of them and by not moving. "Being aware and not moving" means not speaking, not doing anything with the body. Moving either the mouth or body is what Buddhists call karma. When we stop an automatic behavior, when we create a gap between a thought and the action or speech that usually follows it, we are wedging open the door to the prison made of thousands of conditioned habit patterns. Eventually, after years of practice, the door will stand wide open. When the old habit patterns surface, we will have choice. We will even be able to smile at the absurdity of the many schemes of our mind.

EXERCISES

Becoming Aware of Conditioning around Eating

It's useful to begin by recalling what mealtimes were like for you in childhood. Find a partner for this exercise. Describe to your partner a typical meal when you were five to ten years old. Start with breakfast. Later move to lunch and dinner. Your partner can prompt you by asking questions if needed: Where did you eat? Who was present? What was the noise and activity level? Who made the food? How was it served? What was the mood as you ate? What was talked about? Who did the talking? How long did the meal last? How did people get up and leave? As a five- to ten-year-old, did you have any chores around cooking, eating, or cleanup? Now reverse roles so your partner does the exercise while you listen and ask questions.

Ask a person in your nuclear family about meals when *they* were five to ten years old. It's important to ask in a warm and nonjudgmental way, as if you were an academic doing historical research. You can frame this undertaking by saying that you want to gather family history and learn more about your parents' or other relatives' lives.

If you ask a parent or grandparent, you may learn about their conditioning around eating and how it was handed down to you. If you ask a sibling you may get a different point of view on your family's habits around eating.

Tell a partner as many rules around food, eating, and table manners as you can remember from your childhood. For example: "Clean your plate or else _____," "No dessert unless you _____," "Don't chew with your mouth open," "Children are to be seen, not heard."

Tell your partner how you have reacted to these rules. Do you still honor them, or have you modified or rebelled against them?

―――――――

Ask at least one person who knew you when you were five to ten years old what kind of an eater you were. If you are polling a parent or an older sibling, you can ask about your eating patterns from birth through childhood.

Can they describe your eating habits in one word? One sentence? Did you have any physical difficulties around eating? Colic? Gastroesophageal reflux? Stomachaches? Diarrhea or constipation? Were there foods you hated or loved? How did they know this?

Note: This is a slightly risky undertaking, as you may hear uncomfortable things about yourself. Keep in mind that what you hear is only a point of view, and there are as many points of view as there are people. One person's point of view about the you-of-the-past may be flattering, interesting, or upsetting, but it is only a very small part of the truth.

We have to become the scientist and the experimental animal. We have to want to uncover our half-hidden habit patterns around food so we can gain freedom from automatic behaviors. We have to be curious and nonjudgmental about this interesting construction we call "myself."

―――――――

Feast or Famine (Binging and Dieting)

One particularly strong area of conditioning has to do with binging and dieting. If we look at these impulses, we find that they are rooted not only in our personal life experiences but in our collective human history.

"I have been dieting since age fourteen," Curt said. "It has been a grit-your-teeth daily battle for all those years. From the first moment of the day, when I wake up and can't have what I want for breakfast, through the entire day until the evening when I argue with myself about wanting to eat a second dinner, it has been a grim, nonstop battle." Curt found that joining Overeaters Anonymous helped him. "I stopped dieting and became abstinent,* and I lost seventy-five pounds. But then I made the mistake of eating one bowl of ice cream, and I ended up regaining those seventy-five pounds." He says that he struggled again and became "abstinent again," and lost that seventy-five pounds. "But I ate one cookie at a weekend retreat, because they were out on the tea table and everyone was eating cookies, and that cookie became twenty-five more pounds."

This is the feast-or-famine mode of dieting. One "voice" in your mind takes over and puts you on a diet. It talks to you about the rules, the shoulds and should nots. You should eat five small meals, you should skip breakfast and eat only one big meal, protein is good, fat is bad, no, fat is good and carbohydrates are bad. You can have an extra candy because you didn't have real sugar in your coffee this morning but you can't have butter or salt on your popcorn because you didn't exercise at all this week and salt makes you retain water and gain weight.

Sooner or later you get tired of being constantly nagged by this voice and a change occurs. Another part or voice takes over. It might be triggered by indulging in a single cookie or one bowl of ice cream. "What the heck," it says. "You've blown it now, so you might as well go all the way." Suddenly you flip out of the iron grip of strict discipline and into the indulgence of eating what you want, and a lot of it.

Flipping between fasting mode and feasting mode, also called "yo-yoing," becomes a way of life for many people. It is a frustrating, exhausting, and demoralizing way to live. When the inner voice that is not currently in charge has the power to emerge and take over any time, you have to be on guard duty day and night. Who wants to live their life as both perpetrator and victim of an unending internal battle? The Buddha said that it does not matter if we desire something or hate it, we are still tethered like a dog to a stake. If we binge on meat or

---

*Although Curt uses the word *abstinent*, this term applies more to recovery from drug and alcohol addiction than to a food addiction. We have to eat to live. It's important to realize that it's actually much harder to *reduce* your consumption of something you use addictively than it is to stop using it altogether.

if we are a fanatical vegetarian, we are still tethered to the same stake (or steak).

How can we untie the rope that binds us to either desire or aversion toward food? How can we bring ourselves to a sense of ongoing trust with food, to find peace in body and mind when we eat? It helps to look at our hidden impulses through a historical lens.

THE ANCIENT CALL TO FEAST—AND FEAR OF FAMINE

Our ancestors did not have a constant supply of food. When a large animal—a whale, a bison, a wooly mammoth, or an elephant—was killed, everyone feasted, gorged. There was no refrigeration, no way to preserve what was left. After a few days the meat would begin to rot, and it might be weeks or months before another big kill, so large amounts had to be eaten quickly and then stored in the body for the times of scarcity that were sure to come. This is an ancient or atavistic memory that calls us to eat all we can now, even if we are not hungry, just in case there won't be any food tomorrow. It doesn't matter whether or not we personally have ever been without food in our lives or whether our parents and grandparents have always had food as well—there is something deep in our primitive brain that still fears starvation, scarcity, famine.

Famine has continued to be a reality of human life despite the development of agriculture and the technological advances that have increased crop production over human history. There are countless examples of large numbers of people starving to death, both in ancient and modern times. Over three thousand years ago Egypt suffered several decades of drought. An autobiographical text left by one ruler from this devastating era states, "All of Upper Egypt was dying of hunger and people were eating their children." The Old Testament describes seven consecutive lean years and plagues of locusts that ate all the crops in the fields. Walter Mallory, a famine relief officer in Asia, noted that Chinese scribes carefully recorded 1,828 famines between 108 B.C.E. and 1911 C.E., almost one famine each year.

During the last sixty years famines have killed 30 million people in China, 3 million in North Korea, and half a million in Ethiopia. In the twenty-first century, a child dies of hunger every five seconds somewhere on this earth. Of all the continents, only North America seems to have been spared the suffering of widespread famine. However, one in eight American children goes to bed hungry, and one in six elderly people has an inadequate diet. Almost half of the mayors of American cities report that they cannot meet their most vulnerable citizens' needs for food. Fear of scarcity and the instinctual imperative to eat food while we have it are therefore not unfounded even in our own time, and these feelings combine to produce one of our most primitive and powerful drives.

On top of these ancient and cellular fears about starving to death, many more people than you might expect have had actual experiences of scarcity or starvation in their own lives. These distressing memories confirm and reinforce the atavistic fears with a little voice that says, "Remember the time we were hungry before? It could happen again. Better eat what you can while it's in the fridge."

EXPERIENCES OF DEPRIVATION

You might think that no one you know has ever been truly starving, but you are probably wrong. I didn't realize this until I began leading mindful eating workshops and heard stories of early deprivation, even in middle-class families. As participants hesitatingly told their stories to the group, they often had insights into how their self-defeating patterns with food had developed. The younger a person was when these experiences around eating occurred, the stronger the reactive pattern was likely to be. Here are three examples.

Josh's Story

When Josh was six, his father died of colon cancer. For several years before that his father was in and out of the hospital, and family meals were lost in the chaos. After his father died, his mother, an award-winning elementary school teacher, sank into deep depression. She was able to pull herself together for a day of teaching, but she arrived home with no energy left to cook or even to stock the kitchen with food. He recalls her crying continuously for several years before she married again. It was an unfortunate choice, a man who was verbally abusive to her and to Josh. Josh lived on the food he was able to scavenge for himself: peanut butter, canned SpaghettiOs, Froot Loops sugared cereal, croutons from a box, bologna, milk, and Pop-Tarts.

As an adult he says that the foods that sustained him through a lonely childhood are comforting, even dry croutons. He describes himself as "addicted" to peanut butter. He undertook a month of abstinence from peanut butter in order to face his fear of being without it. Through mindful eating practice, Josh has become aware that certain foods can provide solace. He is able to use them with awareness of their particular power, without overeating.

Lydia's Story

Lydia was raised by parents who were teenagers when they conceived her, the first of five closely spaced children. Children raising children. Actually, alcoholic children raising children. Lydia told us that her parents would disappear, sometimes for days, drinking with friends. Lydia was told to look after the younger children. She remembers them crying in hunger, in a house empty of food. She fed them ice scraped from the freezer compartment flavored with vanilla, the only thing she found in an otherwise bare cupboard. Lydia now loves to cook, eat, and feed people. Memories of near starvation keep her safely over three hundred pounds despite many periods of dieting. She has uncontrolled diabetes and high blood pressure and is contemplating intestinal bypass surgery. She knows that after surgery she will have to be very careful about what she eats and that her portion sizes will be very small. In preparation for surgery she is learning mindful eating.

Erika's Story

Erika was born to older parents, with a condition that made her skin rough, flaky, and easily infected. Her rigid, critical mother was unable to care for her and she was placed in an infants' home at six months. There she became ill and was transferred to a hospital, where she was fed through a tube in her nose. The misguided policy at that time was not to allow parents to visit, let alone stay overnight in the hospital, for fear of upsetting the sick child. She didn't return home until she was a year old.

During a long meditation retreat Erika was suddenly transported back to infancy. She vividly reexperienced herself as a small being in a huge, cold bed, too weak to move anything but her eyes. A cold, bright light shone in her eyes. Periodically an adult who smelled bad would appear and touch her with cold hands. She recalls, "I was hollow below the throat and the stomach seemed to be an empty sea of longing."

Erika came from a middle-class family, but her parents disapproved of her career choice, telling her that she lacked the intelligence and stamina to become a doctor. She became an impoverished student, attending medical school in a foreign country. She studied in streetcars because they were warm. She says that her thinking became organized around what and when she could eat. She learned where to buy the cheapest food, and she looked with longing at food left on plates, in garbage bins, or dropped on the floor in grocery stores. She saw many pets given meals that she herself would have wolfed down gladly. She felt envious of people in restaurants, as casual with their food as she once had been. At times, the temptation to take food that people had left behind was "almost unbearable." She discovered new companions, whom she describes as "old bearded beggars, strangely dressed and forlorn immigrants, the lonely elderly carefully dressed and rummaging in garbage cans, the poor mothers queuing up for bargains in the pouring rain."

These experiences have left their mark in suffering, but they also have made Erika a more compassionate physician, able to "tune in to this view of the world any time and have a soft spot for food obsessions." She became an oncologist, caring for those with cancer, the most lonely and frightened patients. Among them are many children, among them are many people who cannot eat and are wasting away.

These are stories, not just of unsatisfied physical hunger but also of unsatisfied heart hunger. Food and love, which are often wedded in our minds, become traumatically bonded when parents deprive a child of both caloric and emotional nutrition.

Because her experience of deprivation occurred earlier in life, when she had fewer coping skills, and because it involved guilt over not being able to relieve the suffering of her little brothers and sisters and anger at her immature parents, Lydia's eating patterns are more likely to be fueled by strong reactive pattern. She might be more likely to gorge when food is available, more likely to urge food on those she loves, more likely to stockpile food. Because Erika was physically hungry as an adult, when she was able to talk herself through a temporary and even noble situation in medical school, she may have a less powerful reactive pattern. She might find herself eating seconds when she isn't really hungry or taking home in her briefcase the little bag of pretzels she didn't eat on the airplane.

I have encountered many examples of food deprivation in my work. There are the children diagnosed with "failure to thrive," small and barely growing despite our earnest nutritional advice to their parents. Suddenly, when they turned two or three, their weight would shoot up. We realized that they were now able to get into cupboards and open refrigerators by themselves, and get the food they needed. Addicted parents who lose their appetites when they are high on drugs often neglect to feed their children. I have talked to many children who began fixing food at age six or seven for both themselves and their younger siblings. Their parents were either high or sleeping off a high, and forgot to feed their children. These children may not have conscious memories of being starved, but their unconscious minds will remember. They may feel a strong urge to eat more than they need to now, in case food is not available tomorrow or all next week. *These early experiences of "not enough" are powerful forms of conditioning. When not enough food is paired with not enough love, the impact is doubly deep.*

HOW TO WORK WITH FEAR OF HUNGER

The ancient fear of death by starvation was so necessary to survival that it seems to have become part of our very cells. When this primitive anxiety, passed on over countless generations, becomes paired in this lifetime with actual experiences of scarcity, powerful emotions can arise apparently out of nowhere, driving us to eat. As long as our behavior is being controlled by our ancestral memories, by our subconscious mind, and by conditioned habit patterns, we are not free. If we try to overcome these by forcing ourselves into a pattern of rigid control we still will not be free.

How can we liberate ourselves from patterns of conditioning that have been repeated for many years, even many generations? We begin with mindfulness exercises. These exercises, and our group discussions about these exercises, can help us discover hidden thoughts and automatic behaviors. Once we bring them up into the light of awareness these behaviors will change. They may change slowly, but they will no longer have the hold on us that they did when they were operating in the darkness of our unconscious, hidden from the light of our awareness.

I repeat, a small change is all that's needed, a small change in awareness, a small change in behavior. The anthropologist Margaret Mead observed that a custom, let's say always eating fish on Fridays, could persist unchanged for centuries in a culture. However, as soon as someone traveled outside the culture and saw that there was the possibility of doing things differently, the old custom was doomed. It might take centuries, but inevitably it would change. People would begin to eat chicken on Fridays, or fish on Tuesdays. This is true of our individual customs, too. As long as our habit patterns are hidden backstage, they will remain unchanged. As soon as we bring them up onto the stage of our mind and shine the spotlight of awareness on them, they will inevitably change.

For example, once we see that whenever we are stressed we soothe ourselves with vanilla ice cream, this habit will begin to loosen its hold on us. The next step is to change our behavior. If we are able to experience the impulse to eat in an unhealthy way and *not act upon it*, even once in a while, this is wonderful. This might mean not having the vanilla ice cream or substituting frozen mango slices or just delaying eating the ice cream for thirty minutes. Do not discount small and intermittent changes in your behavior. Ultimately small shifts can have a big impact, slowly but steadily bringing us to greater health and ease.

EXERCISE
Becoming Aware of Reactive Patterns around Food

With a partner or within a group (or in a journal if you are alone), share stories of:

- Food used as a reward
- Food used as punishment
- Hoarding food
- Deprivation or starvation

Can you discern any reactive patterns that have resulted from these experiences?

EXERCISE
Becoming Aware of Food Cravings, Fears, and Anxieties

You will need a piece of paper and a pen or pencil for this exercise. On the sheet of paper make four columns. At the top of the first column write "Food for Illness." Make a list of foods you would like someone to make for you when you are sick. For example, what do you like to eat when you have a bad cold or the flu? Now, in the same column, write the foods your mother made for you when you were sick. Are they the same or different from what you want today?

At the top of the second column write, "Comfort Foods." List the foods you eat when you need comforting. It helps to ask yourself, "When I drag myself home after a bad day, I think, 'What I really need now is some . . .'"

Title the third column "Craved Foods." Make a list of foods that you find yourself daydreaming about or going out of your way to buy, or foods you never quite get enough of.

Finally, title the fourth column "Feared and Disliked Foods." Make a list of foods that you are fearful of eating or that you particularly dislike. The fear could be felt in a mild form, like avoidance, or a strong form such as distress or even anger when you see or smell the food. Do you know why you dislike or particularly dislike certain foods?

If you are working with a partner or group, take turns reading these lists out loud. Is there any similarity or overlap in different people's lists?

Sugar, Salt, and Fat: An (Un)holy Trio?

Another important aspect of exploring our eating habits is to look into our cravings for what we might call "the big three": sugar, salt, and fat. They are an unholy and very profitable trio. The fast-food industry depends upon our insatiable desire for these three: the soothing taste of sweetness, the tangy taste of salt, and the deep-fried taste and creamy texture of fat. When eaten in excess they play a role in many diseases, including diabetes, high blood pressure, heart disease, obesity, stroke, and fatty liver disease. They have an addictive quality. Witness how hard it is to convert children raised on fast food to a healthy diet. My grandson recently came home from high school lamenting, "They only serve baked french fries at school now and they don't taste as good as deep fried." Out of concern over the epidemic of childhood obesity, the nutritionists in our school district had tossed out their deep-fat fryers. Why does less fat and salt not taste as good, even to a child? Why do fast foods containing the unholy trio taste better than, and thus inevitably displace, traditional foods in every country where they are sold?

It's because sugar, salt, and fat are actually a holy trio. They are essential to our survival. Our body recognizes them as treasured substances. Until recently they were difficult to obtain. The story of our history with these foods will tell us a lot about why they are central to our food cravings and why humans the world over, once they have access to an unlimited supply, become unbalanced in their relationship with them.

Sugar and fat are energy sources. We must have their energy to be a warm and active living being, to run the billions of tiny factories in the cells in our body. Sugar is absorbed quickly and provides an immediate burst of energy, but it cannot be stored in the body for later use. If we are not taking in sugars, our reserves last only about six hours. Fat is absorbed more slowly than sugar and can be stored under our skin and inside "beer" bellies. The body can convert fat into the sugar glucose, making fat a sustained-release fuel. Fat was critical to our ancestors' survival in winter or during lean times. The third substance we crave, salt, is essential to maintain the narrow healthy range of sodium and chloride that all our cells depend on to function. Let's look at our craving for each of the holy trio one at a time.

SUGAR

Why do our mouths desire sweetness? Basically, it's because we can't eat sunshine. We have to rely on plants to convert the sun's energy into sugar, a form we can eat and savor. Sugarcane (in the tropics) and sugar beets (in the temperate zones) are the most efficient converters of energy from the sun into sugar. Sweetness in the form of refined sugar is a recent invention; concentrated sugar has only become available to human bodies in quantity in the last 150 years, as a result of large-scale cultivation of these two plants.

While King Henry III of England had difficulty obtaining three pounds of sugar for a feast, today the average American consumes three pounds of sugar and other sweeteners every week! Only 250 years ago sugar was so valuable in England it was called "white gold." Today, however, King Henry could send a servant to a local grocery with less than two dollars to purchase his three pounds, which wouldn't be enough to make even a few cakes with icing with today's recipes. "Hardly a banquet," modern guests would complain, eyeing a tiny morsel of cake. "Where's the dessert buffet and the chocolate fountain?"

Our first food, breast milk, was sweet, and, given a choice, we choose sweet drinks even before our birth. Babies in the womb swallow amniotic fluid. If sugar is added to that salty liquid, their rate of swallowing goes up. Sweetness also is reassuring to us, a signal that a plant or fruit is likely safe to eat. A bitter flavor often signals that a plant contains dangerous alkaloids.

During most of our 100,000 years of evolution, we humans had to spend a lot of time and energy just to get enough energy to survive. As our brain capacity increased, so did our need for sugar, the brain's fuel. Our human brain comprises one fifth of our body by weight, but it requires more glucose than the rest of our body. Our body can convert starch and fat into glucose, but that conversion requires energy. Pure sugar, a soothing and delicious energy hit, was not readily available to us in olden times. On the rare occasion when people located a stash of sweetness, say a honeycomb, they had to expend a lot of energy climbing the tree, smoking out the bees, extracting the honey from the comb, and healing their scrapes and bee stings. Or they had to tap maple trees, cut wood for fires, and boil a gallon of sap to make a third of a cup of maple syrup. If you add in the energy needed to make the tomahawk to gash the trees and the birch bark buckets to collect the sap and the clay pots to boil it in, that's a lot of work for a third of a cup, or 320 calories, of sweet syrup.

While sugar was rare, we were able to derive great pleasure in a small and infrequent sweet treat. Now that sugar is cheap and ubiquitous, it seems to satisfy us less, and we are consuming more with each passing year. Average consumption of sugar and other sweeteners in the United States is now 152 pounds per person per year, and even higher in Europe and Australia. This is almost a half cup of sugar per day on top of the sugar already present in our food. Most people cannot imagine trying to choke down a total of three-quarters of a cup of sugar or honey, spoonful by spoonful, every day. Yet, we do just this, and quite happily, because sweeteners are hidden in almost all processed food.

One hundred fifty years of exposure to concentrated sugar is only five or six generations, not enough time for human bodies to evolve the ability to handle ten times the sugar intake of our ancestors. It's no wonder our poor pancreas can't produce enough insulin to manage all the extra sweeteners we pour in.

To help me grasp the enormity of the change in our diet since concentrated sugar became cheap, ubiquitous, and a staple in our diet, I took the example of an American Indian woman living 250 years ago in the forest on the banks of the Columbia River where our monastery now stands. What were the sources of sugar in her diet before Europeans first appeared in this land? Fruit. Actually, wild fruit, for this was before white settlers introduced cultivated apple, pear, and plum trees. Native fruit like chokecherries or wild plum were not very sweet. How much fruit sweetness could she enjoy? It depended upon the season. The World Health Organization currently recommends that people eat at least 400 grams of fruit a day. In the summertime a resourceful woman of the local Clatskanie or Chinook tribes would have been able to meet this recommendation if she gathered and ate one cup of blackberries and two cups of wild huckleberries, enjoying a total of 136 calories and 7 grams (1½ teaspoons) of sugar. Most modern women don't pick huckleberries, but they can taste that native fruit in fast-food form by going to a chain called Burgerville and getting a "Northwest huckleberry shake," which contains 790 calories and 105 grams (22 teaspoons) of sugar.

We can't forget that the Native American woman had to expend calories to obtain this sweet bounty. Let's say she had to walk an hour to gather this fruit in various fields and forests. We won't count any calories for picking or processing the fruit. That's an expenditure of 280 calories. The fruit gave her 136 calories, a net drain of 144 calories. Thus she could eat all the "dessert" she wanted and still not gain weight. If you also consider that fruit was only available in the summer, it is obvious why diabetes has become epidemic in modern times, even in children. Human bodies, designed to process a few teaspoons of sugar a day, a few months of the year, cannot cope with modern sugar-laced foods.

If our native woman lived in modern times, she could hop in a car and drive to Burgerville for a Northwest huckleberry shake. A twenty-minute drive plus a few minutes of walking would burn up about 40 calories. After finishing her shake, she would have an extra 750 calories to keep. If she did not burn it in exercise when she got home, then her body would dutifully store it as fat, a hedge against lean winter months to come, and her pancreas would have to produce a lot more insulin to burn the morning's intake of 22 extra teaspoons of sugar. If she drank a Northwest huckleberry shake every day instead of going to the trouble to gather fruit to satisfy her sweet tooth, she would gain about seventy-five pounds a year. Her dentist and her doctor might prosper, but she would not.

Before the industrial revolution, a human body had to work very hard to prevent its own starvation. The primal brain remembers long intervals between successful hunts, long winters with dwindling food stores. Our primal brain demands gorging ourselves when we have the food, before it spoils or we have to flee.

FAT

Over those long winters, when summer's sweet fruit is gone, fat is the fuel we need to burn to stay warm and remain alive. This fuel reserve was critically important to pregnant women and nursing mothers, who had to have enough stored calories during times of scarcity to support their infant's life. You may have noticed that you are hungrier when you are cold. This is an ancient signal from the body saying, "Put on a layer of insulation and store up portable calories for the winter! Food could be scarce!" Restaurants are aware of the power of this ancient signal, and they purposely keep dining rooms cool so customers will order and eat more.

Our instinct to store fuel is the reason we love fat: the creamy fat in crème brûlée, the crispy fat in potato chips, the melt-on-your-tongue fat in chocolate. This is why fast food and many comfort foods contain a lot of fat. Restaurants know that we like to end meals with desserts rich in fat: ice cream, chocolate mousse, cheesecake, anything with whipped cream on top. This desire to finish the day's intake with some fat may have its biological origin in the "hind milk" that comes in at the end of a breast-feeding session. It is extra rich in fat and calories, perhaps nature's strategy to help nursing babies feel full, content, and sleepy (and to give their mothers a break!). It may help us get to sleep, too, to have a warm cup of milk or cocoa before we go to bed.

SALT

Salt, too, appeals to our taste buds because it is essential to human survival. Everyone has tasted the salt in their own tears, sweat, and blood. In hot weather you can feel or even see the salt you are losing in sweat as it crusts on your skin. Under normal conditions we lose two grams of salt a day; while exercising in hot weather it can be more than 30 grams, or 6 teaspoons. Every year military recruits and other people who engage in activity that makes them sweat profusely die as a result of drinking water but not replacing the salt lost in perspiration. Our most vital organs, the heart and the brain, cannot function unless their cells are supplied with adequate salt to maintain certain concentrations of sodium, chloride, potassium, and other elements. While it is critical that our body maintain those concentrations, we have no organ that can store salt. Thus we depend upon a regular supply from the outside to maintain health. When humans were primarily carnivores, they obtained adequate salt from the blood and muscle of their prey. Land plants, however, do not contain enough salts, so when humans began to live in settlements, cultivating and eating plant crops, they had to find sources of supplemental salt. Like the grazing animals, humans beat trails to salt pans or licks. Unlike the other animals, they learned to harvest, refine, and sell this valuable commodity.

Salt is an essential nutrient, a condiment, a disinfectant, and a medicine. It has enabled humans to preserve food, and preserving food enables them to undertake long sea voyages and overland trips—including expeditions to trade salt. At one time salt, like sugar, was worth its weight in gold. Men sold their wives and children into slavery for salt. It became a critical raw material as humans developed skills in various industries including glassmaking, fabric dying, pottery glazing, and leather tanning. Salt is so essential that governments all over the world have depended upon salt taxes to underwrite their budgets and to keep citizens under control; indignation over high taxes on salt imposed by England was a factor in inciting both the American Revolution and Gandhi's fight for India's independence.

Sugar, fat, and salt all have a powerful effect upon our mind states. The following exercise is one of the most revealing that we do in our mindful eating workshops. In it we investigate the effect of food on mood.

EXERCISE

Food and Mood

This exercise can be found on track 5 on the audio CD. Have ready small amounts of sugar, salt, dark or bittersweet chocolate, and hot sauce. (You can substitute small amounts of other sweet, salty, and fatty foods: for example, a half teaspoon of honey, a few salty chips, carob chips, and spicy salsa.)

1. Begin by closing your eyes. Now bring into your mind something upsetting that happened in the past week. Think hard about this event, and purposely stir yourself up by recalling your distress, anger, or frustration. Think about how you would like to get revenge if you could.

    Hint: If you need help generating a distressing recent memory three different times (as the exercise progresses), here are some other possible topics to bring to mind.

    -   Recall something upsetting you heard on the morning news or read in the newspaper.
    -   Recall a time when someone wronged you, cheated you, or betrayed you.
    -   Bring to mind a person who really bugs you. Imagine spending a holiday with them. It could be a coworker, a family member, a politician, or a movie or TV star.

- Bring to mind a time when you were in pain and could not find relief.

Now, on a scale of one (calm) to ten (furious), how would you rate your level of distress?

Next, put a little sugar or honey on your tongue. Savor the taste.

Now, return to the upsetting memory. How would you rate your level of distress? Has it changed?

Now, eat a little more of the sugar with mindful attention.

Return again to the memory. What score would you give it now?

2. Repeat this exercise using salt or a salty but bland food such as plain-style potato chips.
3. Repeat this exercise using a small amount of something fatty such as a square or a few chips of dark chocolate.
4. Repeat this exercise using a small amount of spicy food such as hot sauce.

Remember that there are no "right answers." These are experiments.

This exercise demonstrates why we crave certain foods. They can have a powerful effect upon our moods. We seek out sugar, salt, and fat not only because they were essential and often scarce foods in our ancestral past but because they are potent foods for changing our moods. Perhaps they are potent precisely because they were rare in our historic past, and finding and eating them has always relieved a primitive anxiety related to survival.

Keep in mind: There is nothing wrong with using food skillfully to change a difficult state of mind, if we do it with full awareness and in a way that does not harm our body.

4 | Six Simple Guidelines for Mindful Eating

MINDFULNESS IS A SKILL that can be learned. The ability to be aware—subtly, minutely, and very widely aware—already lies within us. This ability usually lies dormant, accessible only in moments of clarity that we might call "peak moments." But we can learn to cultivate mindfulness, whether in eating or in any aspect of our lives. We can grow mindfulness from brief and intermittent moments of attention to a large and readily accessible field of sustained and clear awareness. In this chapter we'll explore six principles that will help us to cultivate mindfulness as we eat.

1. Slow It Down

In America we eat very quickly. Many people have told me that their attitude toward meals is to "just get it over with as soon as possible." The American habit of eating fast is not new. Foreigners visiting early American taverns recorded their astonishment at how quickly food was eaten. The technique was dubbed "the three G's" for "gobble, gulp, and go." A Tennessee historian records that a European visiting the colonies was puzzled by the "haste, hustle and starving attitude the inn frequenter displayed. Everyone stuffed himself at uncanny speeds." Another visitor "was amazed that in barely twenty minutes he had witnessed two series of meals in his hotel."[1] Our propensity to eat and run has not diminished over the intervening two centuries. Research shows that North Americans spend only eleven minutes eating lunch at a fast-food restaurant and eighteen minutes at a cafeteria in their workplace.[2]

In North America we often eat standing up, or while walking or driving, just cramming the food down on our way to do something else. It's as if we want to get eating over with quickly. We have invented foods for this purpose, like Go-GURT, a yogurt product that we can squeeze out of a tube with one hand so that the other hand is free to drive the car. We can even buy a giant bib to wear as we drive, so our work clothes don't get stained by the food we spill as we munch and swerve our way down the road.

In many Asian and European countries this is considered a shocking way to eat, bordering on barbaric. An European friend tells of meals in France, where just the perusal of the menu and careful consideration of what to select takes at least half an hour. Each possibility must be discussed and questions asked of the waiter. The proprietor of the restaurant and the waiting staff would be insulted if you took a quick glance and placed an order. The cook would be hurt if you ate your food absent-mindedly while talking on a cell phone. A meal is a ceremony, a time to enjoy not just the food, but the anticipation of the food, and the good company. To give the food and drink proper attention is to repay the effort of the people who are serving you. You repay them more with your appreciation than with your money.

In Japan, eating while walking is considered extremely bad manners. Only in the last few years has it become acceptable in Japan to eat while walking, and that applies to just one kind of food, ice cream cones, and only because they will melt. All other foods and drinks are to be eaten while seated and thus given proper attention. There are stores that sell "fast food" such as hot potato croquettes, steamed filled buns, or *furaido chikin* (fried chicken), but the food always is taken home and put on a proper plate, garnished nicely, and eaten with proper attentiveness.

THE ADVANTAGES OF EATING MORE SLOWLY

There are many disadvantages to eating quickly. Some of our satisfaction in eating comes from chewing. That's why we like crunchy or chewy food and why we don't puree all our food and just drink it through a straw. Our mouth enjoys different textures. It feels it has eaten something when it has participated actively, not just swallowed. People who have their jaws wired shut after a fracture can only drink liquids. No matter how much they drink, they usually lose weight. They get tired of milk shakes and smoothies three times a day and are very happy when the wires are removed and they can chew again. Our mouth also enjoys different flavors. When we chew well, flavors continue to be released. A disadvantage of eating quickly is that we barely taste the food, have only a vague experience of what we've eaten, and are very likely to want more.

A nurse told me the story of a woman who had stomach-stapling surgery. After the operation a dietician explained to her the necessity of chewing her food thoroughly because the smaller stomach reacts with pain to large lumps of food. Upon trying this new skill of chewing her food well, the woman exclaimed, "If I had been taught this earlier, I wouldn't have needed the surgery!"

Chewing food well not only gives the mouth more exercise and satisfaction from experiencing changing textures and flavors, but it helps us get more nutrients from what we eat. There are enzymes in saliva that break down food, allowing the mouth to begin absorbing nutrients even before we have swallowed our food, but this enzyme activity will only happen if we actually chew our food and let it stay in the mouth for more than a few seconds. When we "gobble, gulp, and go," we are going against our body's nutritional wisdom. If we chew well and food is broken down into finer particles, it can be absorbed more quickly and easily. It is a kind thing to do for our digestive system. Our body is able to get more nutrition out of less food.

In the early 1900s, a San Francisco art dealer named Horace Fletcher lost forty-two pounds and improved his health by chewing his food well. Soon he had started a movement, persuading thousands of Americans to eat in this new way, chewing each bite of food at least thirty-two times. He advised people to eat only when hungry, to eat only the foods they craved, to stop eating when they were no longer hungry, and to chew every morsel of food until no more taste could be extracted from it.[3]

"Fletcherizing," or chewing each bite from thirty to one hundred times, grew quickly as a fad, especially after a study showed that people who Fletcherized were better able to solve chess problems than those who did not. There were many enthusiastic converts to Fletcherizing, including the writers Henry James and Upton Sinclair, the philanthropist John D. Rockefeller, and Dr. John Harvey Kellogg, the coinventor of breakfast cereal and father of the American health food movement, who taught Fletcherizing at his health clinic in Battle Creek, Michigan.

When we introduce the practice of chewing thoroughly, workshop participants often find it a novel experience. One woman exclaimed, "I realized that I barely chew at all! All my life the food has gone in my mouth and down my throat, almost unchanged." How many chews it takes to process your food well depends upon whether you are eating soup (none) or nuts (lots). Experiment with this for yourself.

SLOWER EATING MEANS MORE SATISFACTION

In addition to knowing when our stomach is hungry, we need to know when our stomach is satisfied. We need an "appestat," a hunger thermostat that registers how much food we have eaten and turns off the heat of our desire for food when we have had enough. A normal appestat responds to four sources of information about satiety. The first signal is the physical sensation of fullness. This message travels from the stretched stomach via the vagus nerve to the satiety center in the hypothalamus in the brain. The second signal comes from nutrients that are absorbed into the bloodstream, including glucose, fat, and amino acids from broken-down protein. The third signal comes from hormones that are released from the small intestine and pancreas as food is absorbed. These include cholecystokinin, insulin, and glucagon. The fourth source of signals are the fat cells themselves. They release leptin and other chemicals that help turn off hunger. (Recent research indicates that the chemicals produced by overabundant fat cells may be harmful to other organs, including the liver.)

If we chew more and our food is broken down into smaller particles, absorption of nutrients can begin earlier in the mouth and stomach. When food exits the stomach and enters the small intestine, appestat hormones signal the brain and body, "We've had enough. We're satisfied. Time to slow down. Think about stopping eating soon." It takes about twenty minutes for this important biological feedback loop to be completed.

Thus, there's an intelligence in eating slowly. First, if we eat slowly, nutrients are absorbed early, in the mouth. Second, chemical signals of satisfaction occur earlier. If we eat slowly we allow food time to reach the small intestine and trigger the "OK, I'm full" signal before we've eaten too much. If we eat too quickly, we've already packed in too much food in before the satiation signal can arrive. Then we don't stop eating until we are physically uncomfortable, which is after we've consumed more calories than our body needs.

In one study, nutrition scientists at the University of Rhode Island offered college-age women a huge plate of pasta with sauce. When the women were told to eat as quickly as possible, they took in 646 calories in nine minutes. When told to eat slowly and put their utensil down between bites, they ate 579 calories in twenty-nine minutes. The group who ate more slowly nonetheless rated themselves as less hungry and more satisfied after the meal, and they also reported enjoying the meal more than the group who gobbled.[4]

Our bodies are designed for eating slowly. Our ancestors didn't have food processors, meat tenderizers, or efficient cooking systems. They had to chew tough meat or blubber, eat partly ground grains and acorns, and gnaw on half-cooked roots and vegetables. If they lived long enough, their teeth actually became ground down. Mothers made their own baby food by chewing food and spitting it into their babies' mouths. It is only recently in our evolution that humans have been able to pack a lot of calories into sustenance that is very easy to find, prepare, and eat quickly.

A woman told me that she had lost thirty pounds in the year after attending a mindful eating workshop. How did she do it? She began to ponder the question, "Why do I eat?" The answer that came was, "To feel at peace." Therefore she resolved to eat only until she felt peaceful inside. No special diet, nothing forced, just slowing her eating down so she could attend to internal sensations of hunger and notice when they changed into sensations of peace. Then stop.

Unfortunately, we are training our children just the opposite, to eat quickly and unmindfully. We buy them fast food to eat in the car as we speed down the freeway between afternoon dance lessons and an evening soccer game, listening to iPods or the radio. I have been amazed to discover that many students in their twenties and thirties grew up in families where sitting down together to eat a leisurely meal occurred only rarely, mostly on holidays. It is common now that kids are given money to buy themselves meals, including dinner, from a fast-food outlet. Even at home, everyone eats by themselves, distracted by their own form of entertainment: watching television, playing video games, chatting on a cell phone, e-mailing, shopping online, or listening to their own iPod.

At our local elementary school, lunchtime and recess combined are allotted only thirty minutes. Most children eat in less than ten minutes so they will have some time to play. This is not unusual. Researchers who observed students' behavior in school cafeterias in four states found that kids spent from 7.3 minutes (New York) to 9.5 minutes (Texas) actually eating their lunches. Different schools allocated a total of fifteen to thirty minutes for lunch. It took students between three and eight minutes to be served and to clean up. What were they doing with their "extra" few minutes? In some cases, these five to ten minutes were their only time for recess or exercise. Some students talked with classmates for a few minutes. In a few schools that allowed a longer time for lunch and required that students stay in the cafeteria, students spent up to twenty-five minutes socializing but did not take any more time to relax and enjoy eating. The study concludes that "a school foodservice director should feel comfortable in stating that students (K-12) need approximately 10 minutes just to consume their lunch."[5]

In 2006, the *Boston Globe* reported statistics from the School Nutrition Association showing that the average lunch period in elementary schools has decreased by six minutes over the last two years. One child said, "Sometimes the teacher brings you down late and you only get five minutes."[6] The *Philadelphia Inquirer* found that local schools served "lunch" anytime between 8:20 A.M. and 2:15 P.M. "Students may not be hungry in the early hours while others are famished by afternoon." They also found that when lunch was scheduled too early students tended to treat it as a snack time and buy junk food.[7] My grandson related that the cafeteria at his middle school in Michigan was so crowded that, not uncommonly, by the time he stood in line to pick and purchase lunch, the bell would ring and he'd have to throw most of his lunch away as he rushed off to class.

If we want to teach children to eat mindfully, it seems that it will have to be done at home. Many of the mindful eating exercises in this book can be introduced to children as games involving everyone at the dinner table. This is one of those times when it is fine to "play with your food"!

The hungrier we, or our children, are, the more important it is to eat slowly and with attention. When we feel that we are "starving," we tend to cram food in quickly, taking in too much before the twenty-minute satiety signal alerts us to stop. We also need to be more mindful when eating comfort foods or favorite foods. You would think that we would naturally eat our favorite food more slowly in order to savor it, but studies show that the opposite is true. The more we like food the faster we chew and swallow it.[8]

There are many ways to slow down our eating and drinking. You might experiment by trying each of the following techniques for one week.

HOW TO SLOW DOWN YOUR EATING AND DRINKING

Make a point of pausing

Here are some methods for helping yourself to slow down your eating by creating pauses:

1. Pause before beginning the meal. Look at each item of food, taking it in with the eyes. Notice colors, textures, shapes, arrangement on the plate or bowl.

2. Take a moment to say grace. Thank the animals, plants, and people who brought this food to you. Be aware of their gifts as you eat.

3. Begin the meal by pausing to inhale the fragrance of the food. Imagine that you are being nourished by just the smell.

4. Eat like a wine connoisseur tastes wine. First sniff the food, enjoying the bouquet. Then take a small taste. Roll it around in the mouth, savoring it. What ingredients can you detect? Chew slowly and swallow. Take a sip of water to cleanse the palate. When the mouth is empty of food and flavor, repeat the process.

5. If you notice that you are eating without tasting, stop and pause to look at the food again.

Fletcherize

The old name for a food blender was a Fletcherizer, after Horace Fletcher, the man who gave public talks in the early years of the twentieth century about how he had lost weight and gained better health by chewing his food well. He recommended thirty-two chews for each bite.

Try chewing each bite of food at least fifteen to thirty times before swallowing.

Watch any reactions to the texture changes in the food as you chew, and pay attention to your reaction to the time it takes to eat this way.

You may want to do this for only part of one meal each day, but as you get used to it, you may find yourself chewing all your food more thoroughly.

The hungrier we are, the more important it is to eat mindfully. When you feel that you are "starving" and "could eat a horse," very deliberately slow down and chew well before you swallow. With each swallow you can say silently, "Dear body, now I'm sending you a present, something very good."

Watch how that feeling of almost desperate hunger changes as you eat. When does it disappear?

Drink slowly

When we gulp drinks, we don't taste them. As a result we drink more, trying to get more taste sensations. We can slow down our drinking in two ways. The first is to enjoy what we're drinking by holding the liquid in the mouth for a few seconds before swallowing it. Swirl it around a bit and enjoy the taste before swallowing. Pretend you are in a TV ad, showing the audience how much you enjoy this drink.

The second method is to put the cup or glass down while tasting and swallowing. Only when the mouth is empty and the taste is fading do we pick it up and take another drink.

Put down the fork or spoon

This is one of the most reliable and simple ways to slow down your eating. Each time you put a bite of food into your mouth, put down the fork or spoon, onto the plate or into the bowl. Don't pick it up again until the bite you have in your mouth is chewed and savored completely and swallowed. For real appreciation of the bite that is in your mouth you can close your eyes as you chew and swallow.

When that one bite has been thoroughly tasted and is gone, then you pick up the utensil, take another bite, and put the utensil down again. Watch the interesting impulses that arise in the mind with this practice. An exercise based on this method of slowing down your eating can be found on track 6 of the audio CD.

Eat with the nondominant hand

In this method you deliberately eat using your nondominant hand. Thus, if you usually use your right hand to hold the fork and put food into your mouth, you switch and eat with your left hand for one week. Watch what happens. It can be quite funny.

I started this practice as a mindfulness exercise, but I do it every day now partly as a way to strengthen my left hand in case I have a stroke. There's a history of stroke in my family, so I figure it's good planning and good exercise for the right side of my brain.

Eat with chopsticks

This practice works to make us slow down and be more attentive to each bite. It works very well if we are not skilled in using chopsticks. It could be one of the reasons that obesity was not historically a problem in Asia. Using chopsticks makes wolfing down a bowl of ice cream completely impossible.

For those who are competent in using chopsticks, or those who want a double mindfulness task, try to eat by using the chopsticks in the nondominant hand. You can also try putting the chopsticks down between bites.

2. Right Amount

The next guideline for mindful eating has to do with how much we eat. The concept of "right amount" comes from the Buddhist teaching of the Eightfold Path to enlightenment. Each part of the path is described with the adjective "right": right view, right mindfulness, right effort, and so on. In the Buddhist teachings "right" means appropriate, beneficial, leading to happiness and freedom. What then is "right amount"?

I first heard of right amount from my Zen teacher Maezumi Roshi. He said that when we considered what was ethical to do in any situation we had to consider several factors: right time, right place, right people, and right amount. I didn't understand the last factor, right amount, very well until I began practicing mindful eating. I saw that mindful eating is ethical action. It is ethical action toward our self, toward all the beings who bring us our food, and toward all those who are hungry in the rest of the world. A country that consumes more than its share of the world's food is a country composed of people who are ignorant of the suffering that results when we are not aware of "right amount." The National Catholic Rural Life Conference is an organization dedicated to the concerns of the rural people who bear the responsibility "for the care of God's creation." They frame nurturing the web of life as a spiritual responsibility, affirming that "Eating is a moral act."[9]

In the monastery our meals are an essential aspect of our spiritual practice. We eat at least one meal a day according to the ancient Zen ceremony called *oryoki*. Except for chanting, we eat in silence, using a special set of bowls. The bowls are graduated in size so they can nest inside each other. Even the largest bowl is not very big. It holds about one and a half cups. *Oryoki* means "just enough." The modest size of our eating bowls helps us eat just enough to remain healthy, just enough to feel satisfied, just enough to meditate without becoming sleepy, just enough to not be swayed by greediness.

"Just enough" is not a fixed amount. It changes according to circumstances. To be aware of "just enough" we have to be mindful. When we practice *oryoki*, we can't take too much, as we must eat everything in our bowls within the time allotted for the meal. We have to be aware of changing conditions, how hungry we are, how much we've been exercising, and how cold it is. The monastery is cold in winter and we need extra calories to keep our bodies warm. A young man who is still growing and has been working all morning digging holes for fence posts needs portions twice as large as a middle-aged person like me. We all adjust how much we take to the amount of food in the serving bowls, the number of people who will be served, and how much food they need to eat.

The beloved Buddhist monk Ajahn Chah gave these guidelines about right amount:

When you think that after another five mouthfuls you'll be full, then stop and drink some water and you will have eaten just the right amount. If you sit or walk afterward you won't feel heavy. . . . But that's not the way we usually do it. When we feel full we take another five mouthfuls. That's what the mind tells us. It doesn't know how to teach itself. . . . Someone who lacks a genuine wish to train their mind will be unable to do it. Keep watching your mind.[10]

As mentioned earlier, these days eating everything on your plate can be bad for your health. "Normal" portion sizes have grown dramatically over just one generation. This increase has occurred wherever food is found, in the portions sold in grocery stores, served in restaurants, estimated in cookbooks, and dished onto our plates at home. Commercially baked cookies have grown to seven times the USDA standard size, and muffins to three times the standard size![11] Our plates and bowls are now bigger, both at home and in restaurants; at antique stores, customers often mistake old serving platters for dinner plates. When we use bigger plates, bowls, and serving utensils, we serve ourselves more and eat more. Many studies show that we eat more food if we use larger containers. For example, if people are given a one-pound bag of M&Ms to snack on as they watch a video, the will eat twice as many candies as people given a half-pound bag.[12] It doesn't matter if we are a six-year-old eating at school or a PhD working in a nutrition lab, faced with larger portions we are all fooled into eating more.[13]

Asian and European visitors tell us they are shocked by the huge portions in American restaurants. Rather than eat too much food, or waste too much food, they may split a meal with a second person. The sizes of portions in fast-food chains located in European countries are smaller than in the same chains in the United States. Portions of all foods in restaurants in France also are smaller, except for salads.[14]

Research shows that up to the age of five, children have a well-functioning "appestat." Even if they are served extra large portions of macaroni and cheese, they eat until they are no longer hungry and then stop. After the age of five children begin to rely on the amount on the plate to tell them how much to eat.[15] They lose awareness of their appestat. In scientific terms, as summarized by the Centers for Disease Control, "Physiologic satiety cues are readily overridden by food cues such as large portions, easy access, and the sensory attractiveness of food."[16] In other words, by the time we enter kindergarten the greed of eye, nose, and mouth hunger begin to override the wisdom of stomach and cellular hunger.

Many adults have ignored the signals from their appestat for so long they have no sense of when to stop eating. They rely on social and visual clues and generally stop eating only when other people at the table have finished eating and the food is gone. Or they rely on painful signals from an overstretched stomach.

Two years after a series of classes on mindful eating, I asked a man who had attended them what he had found useful. He said that he had learned to cut his food into small bites and eat them slowly. His transforming experience in class had been the discovery that one slice of apple eaten mindfully could be as satisfying as an entire apple. (American apple growers are doing their best to obscure this insight. They have placed ads on Japanese TV showing potential consumers, who were used to eating apples as a few slices artfully cut and arranged on a plate, how to "properly" grab and chomp away at a whole apple.)

Zen masters recommend eating until you are two-thirds full. The Okinawans, the longest-lived people in the world, call this practice *hara no hachi bu*, which means "stomach eight parts full." It means never to eat to capacity, to leave a little room in your stomach. A Japanese proverb says that eight parts of a full stomach sustain the man; the other two parts sustain the doctor.[17]

If we followed the advice of the spiritual masters we would maintain mindfulness of the stomach hunger and cellular hunger as we ate, stopping when we were 80 percent full—or at least four or five mouthfuls from being full. Then we would drink some water.

Taking in the Right Amount

This excercise can be found on the audio CD, track 7.

Before you eat, stop to look at the food you will be eating and assess how much you would need to take to be just two-thirds full. As you take a smaller portion and eat it mindfully, reflect, "I am eating this portion for the good health of my body and mind."

Take at least twenty minutes to eat. When you feel two-thirds full, drink some liquid.

Now assess the seven hungers, especially stomach hunger, cellular hunger, and mind hunger. Are they satisfied or not? If one part wants more to eat, why does it want it?

If you take second helpings, reflect, "I am taking this second portion to benefit _____." See if and how the mind fills in the blank.

3. The Energy Equation

Another way to cultivate mindful eating is to become aware of what I call the energy equation. Food is energy. It is actually sunlight, which is converted into plants and then into animals. When we eat, we are taking in the energy of sunlight. When we live our lives, we are releasing and spending that energy.

If our weight stays constant, it is a sure sign that the energy flowing into our body is equal to the energy flowing out. We are in energy balance. If we are losing weight, it means that the energy out is greater. If we are gaining weight, it means that the energy in is greater.

How does the energy flow in? By eating and drinking. As much as we might like to believe that we absorb calories mysteriously from the atmosphere while sleeping at night or just by looking at rich food, it's not true. We ourselves put energy in through our own open mouths.

How does energy flow out? It flows out in all the activities of a human body. These include keeping the body warm, moving the body around, keeping the metabolic factories in all our cells operating, and what is called "insensible loss." Insensible loss includes the energy lost as we exhale warm breath, as we excrete warm urine, when we shiver, and when we have a fever.

ENERGY IN	ENERGY OUT
food	keeping warm
drinks	moving around
	operating the cellular machinery
	insensible losses

If we want to lose weight, there are only two ways to do it. We have to decrease the energy flowing into our body or increase the energy flowing out.

Conversely, if we want to gain weight, there are only two ways to do it. We have to increase the energy flowing into our body or decrease the energy flowing out.

This energy equation may seem obvious, but even well-educated people can be ignorant about it. This equation explains normal fluctuations in our hunger and in our weight. For example, most people find they get hungrier in the fall, as the weather gets colder. The body is burning more calories just to keep a constant internal body temperature. The body is calling for more fuel and also asking that we put on a layer of insulation to protect us from the cold.

If people eat little and exercise feverishly, as often happens in anorexia, the energy balance tips dramatically and they lose alarming amounts of weight quite rapidly.

If we are seriously ill we also lose weight due to the increase in energy out and often a simultaneous loss of energy in. Let's say you have the stomach flu. You are nauseated and the thought of food is revolting. You stop eating for a day. When you begin to feel better you still can't take more than a little warm soup. Maybe you have a fever, which uses calories, or vomiting and diarrhea, which eject calories out of the body. Vomiting and diarrhea are rare occurrences in most people, but they can become a significant flow of energy out. When people deliberately get rid of the extra calories they've consumed by making themselves vomit several times a day or by taking frequent and large doses of laxatives, they put their life in jeopardy.

The energy equation also tells us why we generally gain weight as we get older. In our youth we were active. We walked faster, sat and slept less, and had a higher body temperature, so we needed more calories. As we age we gradually slow down, but we still have a picture in our minds of the right amount of food to eat, namely, the amount we ate when we were teenagers or in our twenties. A once-balanced equation begins to tip in the direction of too many calories flowing in, and we slowly but steadily lose our waists to middle-age spread.

RECENT CHANGES IN THE ENERGY EQUATION

The energy equation explains why so many people in developed countries are now overweight or obese. There has been a marked increase in the energy flowing into human bodies and a marked decrease in the energy flowing out.

MORE ENERGY IN	LESS ENERGY OUT
More-concentrated calories	Less work to obtain food
Cheap, calorie-rich food	Labor- (and thus calorie-) saving devices
Larger portion sizes	More-sedentary lifestyles
More ways to eat mindlessly (for example, eating in cars and while using computers and watching TV)	Entertainment without exercise (for example, driving cars instead of walking; playing video games; watching TV)
Grazing	No gym or recess in schools
Snacking from vending machines	

When most people had to hunt for their food or grow it, they expended just about as many calories getting food on their plates as there were calories in the food on their plates. Think of the work involved in clearing a forest to make a field, cutting down trees, removing brush and stones, and making fences. Then came plowing and planting, hoeing and weeding, watering, more weeding, harvesting, cooking, and preserving. Some crops, such as lettuce or tomatoes, provide fewer calories to a gardener than her body expends to tend them, and are a net calorie drain.

Just getting around used to cost calories. People walked miles to town to buy things they couldn't grow, like flour or sugar. If they were lucky they had carriages, but that wasn't easy, either. It involved building barns, breaking and feeding horses, and making and repairing wagons. Even city life involved exercise. Old apartment buildings did not have elevators if they had fewer than five floors. Can you imagine the complaining today!

Fat cells have one job: storing extra fuel. If we eat it, they store it. If we need it, they release it. The body has no way to get rid of fuel (calories) except to burn them up. It will only burn them if we are in negative energy balance, that is, if we are not taking in all the calories we need for a day's work.

Once we gain extra weight, it is not easy to lose it. Fat cells act like an endocrine organ. You could say that they try to keep themselves alive and full of fat by secreting various chemicals and hormones. If we try to lose weight too quickly, it sets off the body's famine alarm. If we want to avoid setting off this alarm system we should lose weight slowly, about one to two pounds a month. This translates into taking in 100 to 250 fewer calories a day or using up 100 to 250 extra calories a day in exercise.

Small changes work best. In my own life as I've entered middle age this has meant:

- Walking across the shopping center instead of getting back in the car and driving to a second store

- Parking several blocks away from my destination
- Taking the stairs whenever I can
- Not buying candy or soda
- Putting the candy my husband buys me in his office, hidden in a drawer
- Keeping substitutes for ice cream in the freezer, like frozen fruit
- Buying the small package of chips and doling them out to myself one by one
- Taking moderate first servings and looking at why I'm taking seconds—hunger or habit?
- Eating the meal first, waiting a while, and then checking with the stomach and body to decide whether to have dessert and how much to have

EXERCISE

Working with the Energy Equation

Look at the list of small changes above and pick one to try for at least a month. Or create a small change in the energy equation of your own, and try that diligently for a month. Enlist the support of family and friends to remind you of your project or to join you in the task.

At the end of the month, tell someone what you learned from the task. It could be a mindful eating partner, folks in a mindful eating group, or just a friend.

4. Mindful Substitution

Most people are aware that they have many voices in their mind. A childish voice may say, "I want something sweet! I've worked hard all day and I deserve a treat! I happen to know there's a carton of ice cream in the freezer." A parental voice says, "It's only four o'clock. No dessert until you eat a good dinner." An indignant voice exclaims, "Wait a minute! Aren't you about ten pounds overweight? You shouldn't even think about dessert for at least a year!"

How can we work skillfully with these conflicting voices and bring peace to the table? It does no good to stifle them; they just go underground where they can cause mischief. It does no good to indulge them; they just gain strength.

First we become aware of the voices. Each one contains some measure of truth. It could be simultaneously true that you have worked hard and would enjoy a sweet reward *and* that you won't benefit from a jittery sugar high or gaining extra pounds. How to honor both truths? Find a substitute reward.

When we offer the hungry voice a sliced peach drizzled with honey instead of a hot fudge sundae, we are making use of an essential mindful eating practice, that of mindful substitution. When we become aware that there are many voices in our minds—some that are needy, restless, and frightened—we should honor and care for these energies and voices, not in a neurotic, self-absorbed way but in the thoughtful and deliberate way a good parent notices and cares for a young child. This doesn't mean walking out of a tense planning conference at work in order to indulge your "inner child" with an entire Sara Lee cheesecake eaten in a bathtub full of bubbles. It might mean hearing the worried voice inside or feeling the first tendrils of tension in the body and asking for a short break so you can sip a hot drink or suck on a hard candy.

Students have told me about many substitution tricks they have invented. They substitute chewing gum for candy, a chocolate hard candy for a chocolate truffle, the slow ritual of fixing hot tea for gulping a soft drink. One student substitutes frozen mango slices or strawberries for ice cream. Another cuts a piece of cinnamon toast in little pieces and eats them slowly in place of a piece of cake and frosting. Another said that when she becomes aware of a craving for sweets, she gives herself a little snack of something sour, finding that it erases her desire for sweets. She uses a small serving of sauerkraut out of a jar kept ready in the fridge. If that doesn't appeal you could use a few pickles, olives, or kimchi (pickled cabbage). It helps if the flavor is somewhat intense. If you use substitution and then eat mindfully, you get double the benefits.

The point is to take good care of ourselves, the way a loving and wise parent would do. We don't fall into the extreme of angrily scolding and denying ourselves, nor do we lose track of what is healthy and become overindulgent. We steer a skillful but somewhat wobbly course along the middle way.

EXERCISE

Mindful Substitution

When you go grocery shopping, deliberately look for and bring home an appealing but healthy substitute treat like the ones described above. When you feel that you need it, take your time preparing it. Serve it to yourself on a nice plate.

Before you begin eating, assess the seven hungers. Assess the level of satisfaction in your body and heart. Eat the treat slowly, without any distractions. Assess again the seven hungers and the level of satisfaction in body and in heart. If you are working in a mindful eating group, share the substitutions that have worked for you.

5. Out of Sight, Out of Mind

I am subject to what I call "fits of favorite foods." I'll crave and eat one thing, like licorice, for several weeks, and then lose desire for it completely. I used to love chocolate, but a few years ago I developed an allergy to it. Every time I ate chocolate I would get painful blisters in my mouth. I tried every way to get around this sad fact, abstaining for a month, abstaining for six months, to no avail. Even one little chocolate chip could set it off. I felt deprived without my favorite comfort food.

One day I discovered that Reese's Pieces candy had no chocolate! I was so happy that my loving husband bought me a giant bag (cheaper by the pound, right?) and put it in a drawer of my desk. First I had a few pieces, now and then, then a few small handfuls, now and then, and then I had gained five pounds. I stepped back to watch how craving for these candies worked in my mind. I found that when I sat where the bag was in my reach, soon an image of the candy would enter my mind. If I pushed it away, it would return, and return again, until I finally gave in and took a few. The farther away I was from my office, the less often the image appeared and the less vivid or compelling it would be.

I moved the bag to a file drawer in my husband's office, several halls and doors away. I was reluctant to enter his office and go digging for the bag under his eyes. I ate less of the candy, and, with less reinforcement, the colorful candy images appeared in my mind less often. Craving for those little peanut butter delights gradually lessened and finally disappeared. Now I look at them with indifference. They hold no charm.

This kind of solution is supported by eating research. Secretaries who were supplied with free chocolate candies in a glass dish ate the most candies if the chocolates were visible on their desk, less if the candy dish was hidden in a drawer, and even less if they had to walk just six steps to reach the candy. People also eat significantly more if serving dishes full of food are left out on the dining table. If a person has to get up from the table and go back to the kitchen to serve themselves seconds, they tend not to go to the trouble.[18]

The researcher Brian Wansink tells the story this way. A man comes into the office on Friday, hungry because he's had to rush to work with no breakfast. On the way to his cubicle he sees a plate of donuts left over from a meeting the previous day. He pokes a donut and finds that it is hard and stale. He goes to his cubicle, where the vision of the donuts keeps reappearing in his mind. He says "no!" to the impulse to get up and go get a donut. He says "no!" ten times. Finally he gets up and heads for the staff room and the stale donuts. There he meets a coworker who did not see the donuts on his way into the office and has been working all morning without the distracting visions and impulses. Who will eat the most donuts? As Wansink notes, the man who has been struggling with the vision and the impulses all morning will always eat more.

Because the existence of the donuts entered his awareness, because he took in the possibility of eating them and said no ten times, eventually he is likely to say yes.[19]

I once had a striking experience that confirmed this observation. I have never liked donuts. There is something in them that tastes peculiar to me. My first husband loved donuts, so once in a while I'd surprise him on a Sunday morning by going out to get a box of fresh donuts. He liked them and the kids liked them, too, but for myself—I tried bites of many different kinds and finally gave up even trying to like them.

Fast-forward thirty years. I had just finished a workshop and was relaxing as a friend drove me home. We stopped at a corner where people were selling something to raise money for their church. Ever sympathetic toward these kinds of fundraisers, my friend handed five dollars out the car window. Back in came her hand, holding a white box. The box, it turned out, was full of donuts. "No thanks," I said, "I don't like donuts." "These are Krispy Kremes," she said. I had read about the national passion for Krispy Kremes. I was tired and hungry, hungry enough even to eat a donut, so I took a tentative bite. Yum! I took a bigger bite. Creamy and sweet! I could see what the passion was about! I ate one whole donut, then another, and a third. They were really good!

Over the next few days I noticed during meditation that a new window had appeared on the screen of my mind. The window was full of . . . a very enticing KRISPY KREME DONUT! When the thought arose, "But I don't even like donuts!" the Krispy Kreme window would grow larger. "But you DO like Krispy Kremes!" it broadcast. I watched to see what caused the window to appear. I found that it opened when I was feeling anxious, tired, or hungry.

Because I have never liked donuts, and because daily meditation created a certain spaciousness of mind, I had a measure of objectivity. I could even be amused by this window winking open in my mind. Fortunately I live at a rural monastery, an hour and a half from the nearest Krispy Kreme outlet, so I didn't reinforce the sudden appearance of desire by running out to get a donut. I just noted the window as it opened and closed. It took about three weeks for the window to shut and never open again. It helped that I heard a rumor (untrue) that Krispy Kremes derived their creamy texture from glycerin. If the desire for a donut arose, I could counteract it by imagining a donut being injected with mineral oil.

A lawyer told me that he cannot control himself when he eats sweets. He tried many plans for rationing sweet snacks and desserts, but none of them worked. He finally decided not to eat any sweets at all. That worked. He seems at ease with this method, cheerfully turning down cookies or cake without even a second glance. After the first year he decided that he was being too rigid, so he now accepts a small piece of cake at birthday parties.

The practice of out-of-sight, out-of-mind works because anything we do not reinforce will lose its strength. It is a principle of conditioning. If we do not think, speak, or initiate action around something, the force of that thing will eventually wither. This involves active substitution, not forceful resistance, for what we resist can become perversely persistent. For example, when my mind began to conjure up Krispy Kremes, I substituted a more beneficial and interesting mental activity such as a breath meditation, a body scan, or loving-kindness practice. (These exercises will be presented in chapter 5.) When I did not think or talk with others about these donuts, did not run out to buy them, and did not smell or eat them, eventually they lost their hold on me.

FASTING AND MINDFUL EATING

The ultimate banishing strategy for unbalanced eating is fasting. People often ask me about the relationship between fasting and mindful eating. I have no recommendations other than to be sensible and flexible if you decide to fast and to use the tools of mindfulness and investigation of states in order to discover what fasting can teach you.

Fasting leads to some very interesting observations related to hunger and satisfaction. The first observation is that our mind state when we begin a fast has a powerful effect on how hungry we will feel. A technician at the hospital told me that people who have to "fast" on clear liquids for a day before a colonoscopy often complain loudly about how "starved" they are as they arrive for the procedure. On the other hand, people who begin a fast to support a political or religious cause are not distressed by the sensations in their abdomen.

The second observation is that the symptoms of hunger that reoccur at predictable hours are not a mandate from the body about how often it wants us to eat. In fact, the opposite is true. We are the ones who give that mandate to the body about when to feel hungry. Many of us train the body to expect food every six hours, at breakfast time, lunchtime, and dinnertime. If we live in South America and have dinner at 9 P.M., our stomachs won't growl for food at 6:30 P.M.—they'll wait until 9. If we are a Thai Buddhist monk, eventually our stomach won't growl until about 11 A.M., the time for the one daily meal.

MEDIA FASTS

The body feeds on material food, but the mind feeds on information, thoughts, opinions, and ideas. At times the mind becomes full of information that leads to an unhealthy state of mind. For instance, conflicting information about food or diets can lead to anxiety about what to eat or not eat. Perhaps the mind has taken in too much information about the suffering around the world, which leads us to suffer in turn.

Our human mind and heart were designed to deal with the suffering of about fifty people, the size of most human groups during most of the ten thousand years of our evolution. When modern media fills our hearts and minds with graphic images and descriptions of the suffering of hundreds of thousands of people all around the earth, we are likely to be overwhelmed and react with feelings of anxiety and despair. When we are anxious, depressed, or stressed we are more likely to eat in an unbalanced way.[20] Stress can also change how the body processes and stores food, and stress can raise levels of cholesterol in the blood stream.[21]

It can be helpful to undergo a media fast, not reading newspapers or magazines, not listening to the radio, and not listening to the news on the radio or watching the news on TV for a month. Everyone who has tried this has reported that they and their families were pleased with the results. When you decide to begin taking in the news once more, informing yourself again of the thousand ways that people suffer on any given day, regulate the dose. Perhaps you only need to read the newspaper once a week, on Sundays. Never fear, everyone will let you know if something dramatic happens in the world. Does it really matter if you heard it an hour or two later than others?

EXERCISES
Mindful Fasts

Try fasting for just a day or for as long as a week, taking in only juices. (If you are underweight or have an illness such as diabetes, check with your physician first.) Investigate bodily hunger. When does it arise? What sensations is it composed of? Investigate what the mind says about food and not eating.

Try a media fast for at least one week or for as long as a month. Do not watch TV news, listen to news on the radio, or read newspapers, news magazines, or computer news. Use the time for meditation, creative endeavors, or relaxation. Investigate how the mind reacts to this fast. What does it fear?

6. Loving-Kindness and the Inner Critic

When our relationship to eating and food is out of balance, it is easy to be overcome with negative emotions. We may feel aversion to the sight of our body in the mirror, jealousy toward people who can eat "anything they want," or anger toward ourselves for our inability to end our struggle with food and eating. What can we do to counteract these unhappy feelings?

When our mind is full of the voices of conflicting thoughts and emotions, it is hard to do anything in a deliberate and straightforward way. It's like trying to drive a bus when all the passengers are trying to cram into the driver's seat while arguing about where to go! How can we get some distance from these voices and steer the bus of our life down the road of our choice?

The first step is to start a regular meditation practice. Meditation helps to settle and quiet the mind, to create some space around the inner voices. We can begin to sort them out, to hear what individual voices are trying to tell us. (Basic instructions for sitting meditation are offered at the end of this chapter and on the audio CD on track 8.)

When we do this inner listening we may discover a trio of voices that can take over our lives and make us miserable. They love to be put in charge of our eating. We call them inner voices, because you can hear them speaking to you from the "inside." You can hear them arguing with each other about how you should eat. We can name them after their essential functions, the inner perfectionist, the inner pusher, and the inner critic.[22] Each of these inner voices has a specific and rather narrow job description.

THE INNER PERFECTIONIST

The job of the inner perfectionist is to look around for examples of perfection so it can tell you what you should aim for. If you are aiming to be more compassionate, the inner perfectionist might point out Mother Teresa or the Dalai Lama as your role models. If your goal is to become more intelligent, then it will direct your attention to Albert Einstein or Stephen Hawking.

An inner perfectionist that is concerned with the body looks at magazines or movies or people passing on the street and says, "You see that skinny but impossibly large-breasted lady [or that bulked-up hulk of a man]? That's perfection, that's what I want you to aim for." Never mind that the magazine lady's photo has been cropped at the waist and her blemishes airbrushed out. Never mind that the man has been using steroids and spends six self-centered hours a day at the gym. The perfectionist only looks for examples of perfection. It doesn't care how or at what cost perfection is attained.

THE INNER PUSHER

The inner pusher's job is to tell you what to do in order to achieve perfection and then to push you to do it. The inner pusher loves to make lists, long lists of things to do. The inner pusher will nag, cajole, push, and shove, getting you out of bed in the morning and working on its agenda for the day. It is constantly reminding you not to forget what is on your "to do" list(s). It might even have you make a list of your lists. It is never satisfied, so that if you cross two things off the list at night, it adds four more by morning. The inner pusher is aware of which paragon of beauty or virtue the inner perfectionist has chosen and will tell you what you have to do to become like them.

If your wish is to be intelligent, it might tell you that you should get a PhD or at least audit all the relevant lectures at the local university and keep up to date by reading academic journals while sitting on the toilet (your only "free time" if the pusher is in charge of your life). Of course you will have read all the Great Books, some in the original Russian or French. If you wish to become more compassionate, the pusher might urge you to volunteer in a hospice or soup kitchen, or give away your possessions and live among the poor. If you wish to eat "right" and have a healthy body, the inner pusher can set up a tight regimen of exercise and diet for you. When you are reading magazines, the inner pusher is always alert to the latest discoveries and regimens to put on the list.

THE INNER CRITIC

The last of this powerful trio is the inner critic. Its job is to criticize. That's all it does. Whatever comes into its field of vision is fair game for attack by the critic. It is never satisfied, because, as a human being, you will always be imperfect, unable to meet the standards set up by the perfectionist. You will never be as compassionate as Mother Teresa, as intelligent as Einstein, or have a body like the magazine model's. Why? Because the inner critic is not comparing you to a real person, to the real movie star, who actually looks very ordinary without the makeup, the plastic surgery, the skillful lighting, and the photo retouching. It is comparing you to an unreal person, a fantasy person who is coproduced by the media in cooperation with your own mind.

The inner critic has a lot to say about our eating. Remember, its job is to criticize, and the more criticism it can offer, the better it feels about its job performance. A clue that the inner critic is talking in our mind is when we hear the words "should" and "should not." These are the critic's favorite words. For example,

"You should eat less."
"You should not be so uptight about food."
"You should drink twelve full glasses of water a day."
"You should not drink so much, it makes you gain weight."
"You should eat more animal protein."
"You should not eat meat; in fact, you should become a vegan."

You may have noticed, from the examples above and from listening to your mind's own negative commentary, that the inner critic gives contradictory advice. Consistency is not in the inner critic's job description. Remember, its only job is to criticize. It will criticize A and not-A equally. It will criticize you for being mindless about eating, and when you try to eat mindfully, it will criticize you for being too uptight and obsessive about eating. The inner critic is flat, one dimensional. Its only perspective is, "What can I criticize now?"

Except that it's not really "now" that the inner critic attacks. It's a few seconds or a minute ago. The inner critic depends upon comparison, and when we are fully aware in the present moment, when there is no past or future in our mind's awareness, there is nothing to compare. There is only what is, as it is. The inner critic disappears.

This is part of the power of mindfulness. It takes back our life from the tyranny of the inner critic. It brings us to the experience of what is actually true, in our mouth, in our body, now, here, without comparison or criticism. When this happens, it is as if a huge and difficult burden had just been lifted from our shoulders.

When this trio, the inner perfectionist, pusher, and critic, get a grip on any area of your life, they have the power to destroy it. They can undermine your trust in yourself and in others. They can make you stop doing something you love to do. They will suck the life out of your life.

Let's look at how they might work in the realm of eating. If your goal is to eat in a more healthy way, the perfectionist will be reading articles and watching TV with the goal of finding the ideal diet. It will be talking to people who are on diets and listening to experts discussing diets. Finally it will pick one: the Atkins diet, the vegan diet, the macrobiotic diet, the raw foods diet, the South Beach diet.

Now the pusher can move in to implement the diet. It makes lists of the foods and food combinations you can and cannot have and the times you can and cannot eat. It lists places to shop, forbidden foods to get out of your house, books you should read, seminars you should attend, and support programs or electronic mailing lists you should join.

As soon as you begin the diet, the inner critic goes to work. It could even begin to dig at you before you start the diet. "You've failed at all your other pitiful attempts to eat healthy. What makes you think you'll succeed this time? Why even start when we know you are going to fail again?"

If you sidestep that blast and begin your new diet, the inner critic notices how you are falling short of perfection and points it out, not nicely, but with words and tone guaranteed to sting.

"You idiot, you ate grapefruit and grapes together. How could you forget that combination is forbidden on our new diet?"

"Mary Ann is keeping to this diet perfectly and the results show. See the inner glow? You, on the other hand, are failing miserably, and everyone can see it."

"Everyone saw you eating those chips last night, and they're all laughing at you behind your back."

With voices like these on the inside, who needs enemies on the outside?

With inner voices like these, it's a miracle that people can make any improvements in their lives.

Actually—and at times incredibly—these inner voices are trying to help us. Without the inner perfectionist we'd never be inspired by another person's achievements or adopt role models. Without the inner pusher we'd just lie around all day. Without the inner critic we'd never notice where we've fallen short and need to improve. These voices carry useful information, but when they become too powerful and neurotic, their potential for destruction outweighs their intent to assist us.

What if, when we are practicing mindful eating, we hear the voice of the inner critic? Hearing it is just great. Hearing is part of awareness and awareness is the key to awakening. Believing it is the problem.

An essential aspect of mindfulness is to see through these voices, to not be caught or fooled by them. They are driven by fear, and fear distorts clarity. They are not telling us the truth. When you start to practice mindfulness, you notice that there's almost constant chatter going on in your mind—this is true for everyone. Even longtime meditators experience this chatter; they have learned how to quickly quiet it down. The mind is constantly producing thoughts. That's what it does. But we don't have to believe our minds all the time.

Fortunately, there are several ways to work with these inner voices when they get involved with our eating.

EXERCISE

Basic Meditation Practice

Guided instruction in sitting meditation practice is included on the audio CD, on track 8.

Sit down on a chair or on a cushion on the floor. Sit in a way that feels relaxed but upright, allowing plenty of room in the chest and abdomen for breathing. (If you are unable to sit up, you can meditate lying down.)

Focus your attention on your breath. Find the place(s) in the body where you are most aware of the sensations of breathing. Don't try to alter the breath; your body knows very well how to breath; just turn your attention to the breath.

Rest your attention in the constantly changing sensations of breathing for the full duration of the in-breath and the full duration of the outbreath. If you wish, you can be aware of the breath as the spirit of God flowing in and out of you.

Each time your mind wanders away from awareness of the breath (which it is likely to do often), gently bring it back. It is the experience of being relaxed but fully present, as if we have awakened on a vacation day, with nothing special to do except to take simple pleasure in just sitting and breathing.

Once you have been meditating on the breath for a few minutes, you can try one of the other meditation exercises in this book such as the meditation on gratitude for the body.

Work up to twenty or thirty minutes, which is a good amount of time for one meditation session. It is fine to go longer. It is best to meditate every day, making this part of your personal health care or hygiene, like taking a shower (for your mind). On a very busy day you may have to cut the time. Five or ten minutes a day is better than two hours once a month. I find that each minute of meditation is returned two- or three-fold in clarity, equanimity, and efficiency during a busy day.

EXERCISE
Mindfulness of the Inner Critic

Listen for the voice of the inner critic commenting on food, eating habits, weight, and appearance. Listen within your own mind, but also listen as others talk. Be aware of these types of inner critic comments on TV or radio shows.

If you are working with a group, ask others to tell you when they hear you speaking through the inner critic about yourself. An example is, "I'm hopeless at doing these exercises."

Acknowledge the Inner Critic and Let It Go

I learned this method by listening to Mary, the receptionist at our child abuse program. One day she was holding the phone out from her ear and I could hear a screaming voice hurling insults. Mary waited for a pause and gently said, "When you talk that way, it's hard for me to understand you. When I can't understand you, I can't help you."

This is a good way to speak to your inner critic. When you hear an inner voice saying something negative about your eating or your body, you silently say something like, "I know you are very worried about me, but the language you are using isn't helping me. In fact, it makes it harder for me to keep working on the very issue you are worried about. What I need now is kindness, not criticism. Thank you for sharing and good-bye."

Return to awareness of what is occurring in the present moment. Become aware of the in- and out-breaths. Become aware of sounds. Become aware of the many tiny touches on your skin.

Remember, if you are in the present moment, the inner critic cannot speak. The inner critic depends upon past and future, upon comparison.

The Computer Model

Include the inner critic in the field of awareness as you eat, but don't let it take center stage. Let center stage be full of all of the sensations of eating: colors, smells, tastes, textures, sounds. Down in the corner of this large screen of awareness, like a computer screen, is a tiny icon called the inner critic. This is an odd icon, because it can open itself back up and fill up the whole screen of mind awareness.

When you notice that the inner critic has taken over the mind-screen, gently shrink it back down to its proper size and place again.

Loving-Kindness: A Spiritual Antidote

The inner critic is composed of aversive energy, of anger. Anger, and its milder cousin, irritation, are called afflictive emotions because they afflict us—they cause suffering for us and for those around us. They flavor our thinking with a certain sourness and color our world cloudy and dark. The Buddha prescribed specific practices for different afflictive emotions. For the affliction of anger or aversion he prescribed loving-kindness practice. This exercise is on track 9 on the CD.

The practice of loving-kindness (called *metta* or *maitri* in the Buddhist tradition) can be done toward the body as a whole or toward particular parts.

Sit in meditation for a few minutes, letting the breath settle.

On the out-breath, silently say the phrase, "May my body be free from fear and anxiety."

(If you are a visual person you may imagine yourself as free from fear and anxiety.)

Repeat this silent voicing on each out-breath until you feel ready to change.

Change the phrase to, "May my body be at ease."

(Again, you may imagine yourself at ease.)

Repeat this on each out-breath until you feel ready to change.

Change the phrase to, "May my body be happy."

(If you wish, you can imagine this happening. A slight inner smile helps.)

Repeat this on each out-breath until you feel ready to stop.

You can tailor these phrases to your particular situation.

For example, if you are very anxious about eating, you can change it to, "May I be free of fear and anxiety about eating."

Expanding the Field of Loving-Kindness

When we are anxious, our field of awareness collapses into a small box, the box of "me and my troubles." Once we realize that we are stuck in a small box with "me" at the center, it can be helpful to do loving-kindness practice for others.

It is very important, however, to begin with loving-kindness toward ourselves. In Western society people are often reluctant, or "forget," to do loving-kindness for themselves first. They seem to believe that it is a form of selfishness. Actually it is the opposite. Unless we fill up first, renew the pool of loving-kindness in and toward ourselves, we won't have much to give away.

I repeat, it is important to begin with a period of loving-kindness toward ourselves. After some interval, as brief as three minutes or as long as several days, you will feel ready to turn *metta* practice outward.

You can expand the field of loving-kindness by category, breathing and saying the loving-kindness phrases for people of different groups. For example,

"May all people with distress over food and eating be free from fear and anxiety."

"May all people with bulimia be free from fear and anxiety."

You can expand the field of loving-kindness geographically: "May all people in this city with eating problems be free from fear and anxiety. May they be at ease. May they be happy."

As you say each phrase you can envision this happening and see the person or group relaxed, at ease, and happy.

Frequently Asked Questions

As people begin doing the mindful eating exercises and begin making these six guidelines part of their daily lives, some questions naturally arise. Here are some of the most common questions, along with my answers and suggestions.

I like the idea of mindful eating, and I'm convinced that it would really help me with my food issues. But when I sit down to actually try it, I find that I just can't do it. I end up reaching for a distraction like a magazine, the radio, or the TV.

It's not so easy to change our old habits. Begin with small steps, being present with the sensations in the mouth for the first three sips of a drink or the first three bites of food. Next, try to be present for the last few sips or bites. Small intervals of mindful eating will gradually grow into a more cohesive awareness. Also, the guided meditations on the CD can be a big support at first.

When I try the exercise of eating a small piece of food mindfully, taking plea-sure in how it looks, smells, and feels in my mouth, I find that pretty quickly my mind wanders. I can't really stay with the experience for very long.

Like all new skills, mindful eating takes practice. After you've used the guided meditations on the CD a number of times, you will develop your own "voice," an interior guide that gently reminds you to return to full awareness of eating. The mind wanders and returns, wanders and returns. This is normal. Try putting the spoon or fork down between bites. Each time you pick it up again, enter full awareness: looking, smelling, lifting, opening the mouth, chewing, tasting, swallowing.

Mindful eating comes a lot easier to me when I'm eating alone. How do I do this when I'm eating with others?

This is true for anyone. It is much easier to practice mindful eating at first when there are no distractions. When you are with others, let them know that you are trying to relax and be present as you eat. Ask them to help you with a few minutes of silence at the start of the meal so you can really appreciate the food. Assess the seven hungers and savor the first tastes. When a new dish or dessert arrives, do this again. You can make a cook very happy when you truly enjoy the food he or she has prepared.

Next you take on a more challenging task: being aware of two things at once, namely, listening to conversation and paying attention to what is in your mouth. You will find that it is almost impossible to talk and be fully aware of eating, so you will end up doing a lot more listening than talking, both "listening" to your inner companions—your mouth, stomach, and body—and also listening more carefully to your outer companions.

Now that I'm exploring mindful eating myself, I'd like to pass this along to my children. What are the best ways to make mindful eating part of family life?

Here are a few guidelines:

- Eat together, ideally once a day, or at least once a week.
- Say grace or at least thank you to the cook before you eat.
- Have a few moments of silence before eating, and ask your family to be aware of the colors and smells of the food on their plates.
- Ask questions about the food. For example, Where does bread come from? How many people can they imagine were involved in bringing it to our table?
- Try a new food by doing the basic mindful eating exercise with the whole family (this exercise can be found at the end of chapter 1 and on the audio CD, track 2). An Asian or Indian food market is a good place to look for unusual fruits or crackers.
- Do some research and talk about the history of a new fruit or food.

- Introduce your children to the seven hungers.
- Respect their natural appestats by not forcing food. At the same time, encourage them to try at least one bite of a new food and tell you about what they see, smell, taste, and feel in their mouths.
- Relax, have fun, and be curious with your children as you eat.

5 | Cultivating Gratitude

IT IS IRONIC that in countries where food is abundant, disharmony with food and eating is most common. Americans appear to have a particularly unbalanced and often negative relationship with food. In the 1990s, a research team led by an American psychologist and a French sociologist teamed up to do a study of cross-cultural attitudes toward food. They surveyed people in the United States, France, Flemish Belgium, and Japan. They found that Americans associated food with health the most and pleasure the least. For example, when Americans were asked what comes to mind when they hear the words "chocolate cake," they were more likely to say "guilt," while the French said "celebration." The words "heavy cream" elicited "unhealthy" from Americans and "whipped" from the French. The researchers found that Americans worry more about food and derive less pleasure than people in any other nation they surveyed.[1]

Access to ever-increasing amounts of information about food and health seems to be making us feel even more fearful and fraught. A desperate patient once told me,

I'm obsessed with food because I know too much. I can't eat swordfish because of high mercury levels. Tomatoes and potatoes might make my arthritis act up. I've heard that peanuts might be contaminated with a toxic fungus, and tofu and all soy products contain too many estrogens and might lower my sex drive. If I consider the impact of my eating habits on the environment and eat only what's in season, I'm left with little to eat. I also worry that the few foods I might be able to eat have some hidden problem I don't know about yet.

Such pervasive distress about food and eating is a disease only found in people living in an affluent society. It is not a disease of the body but of the mind. It is fueled by information overload, by listening to scientists and advertisers rather than learning to listen to our own bodies.

When I taught in a poor country in Africa, the staple food in homes and in our college cafeteria was thick cornmeal mush heaped in a little mountain on a plate with a dollop of peanut or vegetable sauce poured over the top. If you were well-off, you might have some bits of meat or fish added to the sauce. This is what people ate every day. If you could eat it twice or three times a day, you were affluent. I never encountered people with disturbed eating habits. They were cheerfully grateful just to have enough to eat that day.

Somehow, when we have too much, something happens to our sense of gratitude, and when we lose touch with gratitude, we become increasingly dissatisfied with our lives. We can do several practices, however, that will uncover, at the center of our being, a humble and natural feeling of gratitude for our food and for our underappreciated bodies.

Gratitude for the Body

Most of us take our bodies and our good health for granted. In fact, we don't actually experience ourselves as "healthy" until we fall ill. If we've been sick in bed with a bad cold or the flu, too weak to get up or too nauseated to eat, it seems like a miracle when we begin to recover. For a few days it feels wondrous just to walk, to have an appetite, and to enjoy the smells and tastes of food again. If we've been in severe pain, and it lifts, it can make us euphoric. Very soon, however, we go back to expecting our body to function well, to do what we ask it to do, efficiently and without discomfort.

When someone our own age becomes seriously ill or dies, it lifts the veil of denial, opening our eyes to the impermanence of health and life. We see clearly for a moment that health and life are temporary gifts, and then soon we forget it again. When we forget, we fall back into irritation at our body when it doesn't function perfectly. Why is my hearing going bad? Why does my back hurt? Why do I have allergies when other people don't? Why is my skin getting wrinkled so soon? How could I have gained weight?

Rationally we know that it is inevitable that our body will not function perfectly all the time and we will become ill. It is easy to fall into a critical, anxious attitude about the state of our body, or parts of it, when it fails to perform to our expectations.

When I catch a cold I often feel a sense of impatience, and there's voice inside me that whines about the stupidity of my own medical profession because it can't come up with a treatment for this common affliction. Other voices desperately try to search out the reason I caught a cold this time. Sneezed on by a sick patient? Forgot to take my vitamins? Immune system compromised by stress? What is wrong with me, it asks, that I got sick?

The answer is, nothing is wrong. Your body being sick simply means that you are a being with a body. It is easy to become upset with our body when we have a cold, or indigestion, constipation, food sensitivities, gas pains, irritable bowel syndrome, anorexia, bulimia, diabetes, high blood pressure, asthma, acid reflux, or when we just gain weight. We feel that our body has betrayed us.

We may not be aware of our irritation or anger at our body, but the body is aware of it. If an illness or disability lasts or becomes chronic, then we can be bathing our body continually in the negative energy of our distress. An atmosphere of love and kindness is essential if living beings, including children, pets, plants, and our own bodies, are to thrive and reach their highest potential. When various parts of our body are in trouble, they need extra help and extra kindness, not extra criticism.

Far from failing us, the body actually does an astounding job. Millions of cells in dozens of organs work continually, night and day, without pausing or taking a rest for the entirety of our life. Thought is energy, and negative thought ("I hate my pudgy thighs," "I hate having a sore throat," "I hate my crooked teeth") has a negative effect. All living things wither under the energy of irritation and anger. All living things prosper under the energy of loving-kindness.

There are tools to help us develop mindfulness with our body, to feel and hear its messages from the inside, and then to direct the positive energy of gratitude and loving-kindness toward it. These meditations have the added benefit of helping us tune in to the signals of cellular hunger and also to the body's signals of satiation and satisfaction.

MINDFULNESS OF THE BODY

The Buddha taught mindfulness of the body as a fundamental practice, one that would yield good results for our entire lifetime. He called it meditating "on the body as a body."[2] In Western Buddhist practice, we often meditate this way by doing a "body scan."

At our Zen monastery we begin each day with this meditation. Why? During the night the body and mind become disconnected. Our body is lying in bed asleep, breathing and moving on its own. Our mind is off in its own worlds, dreaming and moving about in other places and times. When we first arise the body is not fully inhabited by our mind, and we stumble about clumsily for a while, until these two can get together. To bring the body and mind together for the work of the day, each morning we use the awareness function of the mind to do a body scan meditation.

EXERCISE

The Basic Body Scan Meditation

This exercise is included on the audio CD, track 10. In this meditation, we start from one end of the body, either the top of the head or the tips of the toes, moving our awareness sequentially through each body part. Our mind is used like a flashlight beam, a light we can direct toward one area at a time.³ As we focus on a part, we open our awareness to all the sensations arising in that part, including:

1. temperature (the spectrum from warm to cold)
2. touch (the many touches on the skin and inside the body, from barely to very noticeable)
3. pressure (from light to very firm or even uncomfortable)
4. movement (a linked series of sensations)
5. the quality of a sensation (sharp or dull, prickly or smooth, constant or intermittent).

We fill our awareness with all of these sensations. After a few seconds or minutes, we move the spotlight of awareness to the next part of the body. The body scan can be done quickly, sweeping through the body in the space of one out-breath. It can be done quite slowly, taking an hour or more to go through the entire body one time.

When you do the body scan meditation, make sure to include the internal organs, such as the lungs, the stomach, the liver, and the kidneys, even if you can't actually feel them. Be sure to include the heart and the brain.

Notice any aversion, irritation, or withdrawal from certain organs or parts.

EXERCISE

Hakuin Zenji's Soft Butter Meditation

The Zen master Hakuin (1686–1768) developed what he called Zen sickness as a result of practicing meditation ferociously, "forsaking food and sleep altogether." He met an old hermit who prescribed several practices that eventually restored Hakuin Zenji to health. One of these was a variation of a body scan called the "soft butter meditation." Here are the hermit's instructions. You may wish to try them.

> Imagine that a lump of soft butter, pure in color and fragrance and the size and shape of a duck egg, is suddenly placed on the top of

your head. As it begins to slowly melt, it imparts an exquisite sensation, moistening and saturating your head within and without. It continues to ooze down, moistening your shoulders, elbows, and chest; permeating lungs, diaphragm, liver, stomach, and bowels; moving down the spine through the hips, pelvis, and buttocks. At that point, all the congestions that have accumulated within the five organs and six viscera, all the aches and pains in the abdomen and other affected parts, will follow the [mind] as it sinks downward into the lower body. As it does, you will distinctly hear a sound like that of water trickling from a higher to a lower place. It will move down through the lower body, suffusing the legs with beneficial warmth, until it reaches the soles of the feet, where it stops.

The student should then repeat the contemplation. As his vital energy flows downward, it gradually fills the lower region of the body, suffusing the body with penetrating warmth, making him feel as if he were sitting up to his navel in a hot bath filled with a decoction of rare and fragrant herbs that had been gathered and infused by a skilled physician.[4]

EXERCISE

Mindfulness Meditation on the Body with Gratitude

This exercise is included on the audio CD, track 11. This is just like the basic body scan, with one difference. After you have focused your awareness on a body part, and just before moving on to the next part, say silently, "Thank you [body part] for [fill in the blank]." Let whatever arises in the mind fill in the second blank. If nothing arises, that's fine.

If, for example, you have focused awareness on the chest and lungs, you become aware of all the sensations coming from the area of the chest and lungs. You are aware of these sensations as they arise, persist, and then fade away. Rest your awareness here as long as you like.

Before moving on to another body part you say silently, "Thank you lungs for . . ." and you allow a little gap. See if any thing arises in that gap. If nothing arises in the gap, that's OK too. Let's say what arises is "for breathing for me all these years, even at night when I'm asleep." Then you move your mind's awareness on to another body part, perhaps the heart.

As you repeat this meditation, try including body parts that you missed in earlier sessions. These might be internal organs like the bowel or small parts like eyelashes.

As you do this meditation, pay special attention to body parts for which you detect some negative energy. Include parts of the body you don't like, such as wrinkles, abdominal fat, or a big nose. Include body parts that are having difficulties.

EXERCISE

Mindfulness Meditation on the Body with Loving-Kindness

This is just like a body scan, with one difference: as we bring awareness to each body part, we send it loving-kindness (*metta* or *maitri*). Traditional *metta* practice involves silently saying the following phrases, directing them first toward oneself, then moving outward in ever-widening circles to include the entire universe.

May you be free from suffering.
May you be at ease.
May you be well [or happy].

In this case we direct the phrases inward, toward the parts of our body, the inhabitants of our inner universe. Here are examples of phrases to direct to body parts on the out-breath. (You may wish to create your own phrases according to the condition of your body.)

May you [name body part or organ] be free from tension and distress.
May you [name body part or organ] be at ease [or satisfied].
May you [name body part or organ] be well [or happy].

Gratitude for Our Food

When food and drink are abundant, it is easy to take them for granted. When we take them for granted, it is easy to stop paying attention to what is on our plate or in our mouth. When we stop paying attention, we stop smelling and tasting. We might as well be eating cardboard. Cardboard is not very satisfying to eat, so we try eating more. When eating more doesn't make us feel satisfied, we try turning up the intensity of taste sensations. We begin with plain potato chips and end up with one hundred varieties calling out to us from the supermarket shelves. We can't decide: Should we have the thin-cut, the thick-cut, the crinkle-cut chips? Should we have the cracked pepper and lime flavor, the sea salt and vinegar, the jalapeno and cheese, or the salsa and sour cream? The bottled drink aisle raises the same anxiety of too many choices. Should we buy spring water from artesian wells or glacial springs, from Colorado, California, or Switzerland? Should it be fruit flavored? Sweetened? If so, with what? Sugar, honey, high-fructose corn syrup, chemical sweeteners, or Stevia?

What happened to the taste of plain water? When we are really thirsty, the taste of plain water is heavenly. As it flows into our dry mouth, it fills us with a simple happiness. This happiness is the opposite of the anxiety of endlessly seeking and never being satisfied. Imagine you haven't had anything to drink for a few days. How grateful would you be to the person who gives you a glass of water? Or imagine how grateful you would feel for a cup of plain water if you were the one who had to dig the well, line it with stones, and pull the water up hand over hand, one bucket at a time? How grateful would you be for a slice of bread if you had to weed and plow the field, sow and raise the grain, grind and sift the flour, and cut and burn the wood in order to bake one loaf?

We have all known the warmth of this kind of simple gratitude for food and drink. When it is lost to us, how can we reclaim it? These days we don't have to perform these many labors before we can eat a piece of bread, but *someone* does. When we cultivate a remembrance of these innumerable someones, our natural sense of gratitude begins to reawaken.

At our Zen monastery, we chant short verses, or *gathas*, before meals. One of them is, "Seventy-two labors brought us this food. We should know how it comes to us." This reminds us, no matter how hungry we are, to pause before eating and reflect upon the life energy that went into bringing the food to the table before us. (Traditionally there are seventy-two jobs that must be done to maintain a monastery, to keep it open and accessible.)

Through mindfulness, we can look more deeply into everyday things. It is an aspect of wisdom not to be fooled by superficial aspects of things, even of the most ordinary things, things that we encounter many times a day. Food is one of these.

When doing mindful eating we can take time to really look at our food. We can appreciate the colors, shapes, and play of light and shadow. This is the way we nourish ourselves through the eyes. However, there is another way of looking while eating. We call it looking deeply into our food.

For most people in our workshops, their introduction to mindful eating comes when they are instructed, step by step, in how to eat just one raisin (see chapter 1). Later we do a different exercise with just one raisin. We look into the life of that single raisin and try to see all the life that has touched it. We call this looking deeply into our food. This looking involves a different sense than our ordinary eyes. It involves seeing with the inner eye.

At Plum Village, the Zen practice center founded by Thich Nhat Hanh, before meals they say, "In this food I see clearly the presence of the entire universe supporting my existence." The following exercise helps us to begin to see how it could be that the whole universe is actually present and supporting us in our food.

Looking Deeply into Our Food

This exercise is on track 12 on the audio CD. You will need one raisin for this exercise.

Pick up the raisin and hold it in your hand. Look at it with your physical eyes. Notice colors, shapes, surface texture, light and dark.

Now imagine that you can see into the raisin and see its history. It is like seeing a videotape of the raisin's life, but it is running backward.

For example, you see how the raisin was placed in your hand. You see where it came from before that, perhaps a bowl, and before that, a box. You see the person who opened the box and shook the raisins out. You see the person who bought the raisins and placed them on the pantry shelf. Before that you see the store, and you see the clerk who unloaded the cartons from the delivery truck, opened them, priced the smaller boxes of raisins, and put them on the shelf in the grocery store.

Next you follow the truck back to the raisin-packing plant, and then, another step back to the drying grapes. Keep going backward, looking with the inner eye at all the living beings, people, animals, and plants, whose life energy flowed into this raisin and into getting it to your hand. When you reach the grape plant, ask where it came from and continue to extend your vision backward in time. Go as far as you can, back through ancestral vines and countries.

Now we ask some questions.

- How many people were involved in bringing this one raisin to you?
- If you include all the animals, plants, insects, worms, and microscopic organisms that had a role in the life of this raisin, how many would there be?
- How far back in time does the life of this raisin go? Where did the carbon, the hydrogen, the iron, in this raisin originate? How old, then, is this raisin?

- Now consider the life energy of all the beings who contributed to the life of this raisin, and, thus, when you eat it, contribute to your life.
- How can we repay them all? Before you read on, please consider, and if you are in a group, discuss this question.

One answer is by eating mindfully. When we eat and look deeply into our food, our hearts reach out to the many forms of life that are sacrificed every day so that we might live more abundantly. How can we repay them? By being alive to them and to the food we eat, which they have provided. By sending them the energy of loving-kindness. By looking deeply into our food and allowing gratitude to arise naturally.

EXERCISE

Loving-Kindness for the Beings Who Brought This Food

Holding in the awareness of your heart and mind the countless beings whose life energy flows into you as you eat, send them loving-kindness. On the out-breath, say silently, "May they be at ease. May they eat and be well satisfied. May they be happy."

---

6 | Conclusion: What Mindful Eating Teaches Us

WHEN WE MAKE mindful eating a regular part of our lives, we benefit in many ways. Not only do we find greater balance and satisfaction with food, we can also discover some of life's most valuable lessons. In this chapter we'll explore some of the deeper lessons and teachings that flow out of mindful eating.

It's OK to Be Empty

Do you think there is something wrong if you feel hungry? Do you keep emergency stashes of food in your purse or briefcase, your car, or your office drawer, just in case your stomach starts to growl? I do. I have three-year-old mints in my purse, covered with fuzz, and a stale energy bar in there, too, just in case my plane crashes and I'm washed up on an uninhabited sandy island or if I'm abducted by terrorists who are impolite enough to forget to feed me at my regular mealtimes.

In this culture we seem to be very uncomfortable with the collection of sensations that we call hunger or thirst. We keep a drink always at hand. We snack all day long. We say, "Actually I'm not very hungry," and proceed to eat an entire meal, in order to make sure that we won't feel hungry later. When we become aware of the intense energy behind this constant filling behavior, we have to ask a question.

Am I willing to be empty?

This is not just a question about how your stomach feels when you haven't had a snack for at least an hour. It is also a question about your whole life.

Let's look at this emptiness question on the physical level first. We eat as though we are afraid to be empty. Between our three full meals, we have snacks or drinks. Maybe the only time we aren't either eating or drinking or at least thinking about eating and drinking is when we are making love or when we're asleep.

What are we afraid of? Are we afraid of the sensations in an empty mouth? Of the sensations in an empty stomach? There is a very interesting mindful eating practice that consists of noticing the physical sensations that we call hunger and thirst arise and then watching the impulses that quickly arise ("Do something!") to change them. When we feel sensations of emptiness, we usually move quickly to put an end to them. We stop at a 7-Eleven, drive up to a fast-food window, or take a coffee break.

I remember a time when people in North America ate three separate meals a day. When you ate, you sat down at a table and talked with other people. There were distinct intervals of up to four or six hours in which you did not eat or even drink. When you were done with a meal, you went back to work, to schoolwork, or to play. Schools and offices did not contain vending machines. Most children brought their lunches from home. If you were "lucky" you had money to buy a hot lunch from the stout cafeteria ladies in white dresses, sensible shoes, and thick black hairnets.

Grazing, the phenomenon of continuous eating, did not exist. It was not supported by the environment, at home, at work, or in school.

When more women began working outside of the home and packaged foods became common, single-serving sizes of snacks appeared on the shelves of supermarkets and convenience stores. Kids quickly discovered these treats, thanks to television, and began to beg for the snack bars, little packs of cookies, bags of chips, and individual cups of colored Jell-O that "all the other kids" had. Unless a mother was poor or aware of nutrition, kids got their prepackaged snacks.

I remember when cars did not have snack trays and cup holders.

Once convenient snack-sized packaging become common and the packages could be tucked into a backpack, a glove compartment, or a purse, food was always at hand and grazing began. Once grazing began, we seem to have become uncomfortable with the sensations from a mouth that was not tasting something and from a stomach that did not contain something. Once fast-food drive-through service became ubiquitous, we could avoid hunger that might arise during the commute between work and home. Once supermarkets introduced sit-down tables next to the deli section, we could avoid any hunger that arose while we were shopping for groceries. Once personal water bottles became necessary for surviving a two-block walk, we could avoid the sensations arising in a mouth that had not had liquid introduced into it for the last five minutes.

Thus, over a single generation we humans have developed a new form of suffering. It is a discomfort, a restlessness, a dissatisfaction that arises if you have not eaten or drunk something in the last half hour. Sometimes you can detect this feeling of unease if you do not have a cold soda can or a warm mug in your hand or a water bottle within reach. Sometimes you can detect this feeling of unease when you realize that there are no more snack packages in your desk drawer. Sometimes you can detect this feeling of unease when you are driving and find that there are no munchies in the glove compartment or no Starbucks in this part of town.

Is it OK for you to feel empty? Most people would probably answer, "No." They like the feeling of fullness in their abdomen. It is comforting. As they investigate mindful eating, they may discover that when they feel empty, fear arises. They may find that they are eating and drinking all day long in order to avoid this feeling. They are imprisoned by the desire for the mouth and stomach to feel full.

Some people, however, would answer, "Yes, I like feeling empty." For them, the feeling of emptiness in their abdomen is pleasant. The feeling of fullness may be unpleasant. After eating they may vomit, purge, or take enemas in order to empty the body and get rid of the feeling of fullness. They are imprisoned by aversion to the feeling of being full.

Other people would answer, "I don't know." They are unaware of whether their stomach or body is signaling hunger. They eat by the clock or they eat when and how much the herd eats. They are imprisoned by ignorance.

As I mentioned earlier, the First Noble Truth of Buddhism is the universality of suffering. If you are a human being, you will encounter suffering in your life. Many people in industrialized countries hear this and think, "This truth of suffering doesn't apply to me. I'm not in a war zone, I'm not being tortured or starving." The suffering that the Buddha talked about, however, is an experience that is often much more subtle than outright pain. It is a feeling of dissatisfaction, a persistent feeling that things are not as they should be. It is an unpleasant or irritating feeling, one that impels us to move, to do something, to distract ourselves, to eat something, to drink something, to binge, to vomit, to make the feeling of dis-ease go away.

Moving away and creating distractions are not long-term solutions to this feeling that something is not right. It is a feeling based in truth. It must be attended to. Eating, drinking, using drugs or alcohol, courting danger, courting a new lover—these are all over-the-counter remedies for temporary relief of this fundamental dis-ease, the intuition that things are not as they could or even should be. The true source of this dissatisfaction is spiritual, and thus the only true cure for it is also spiritual.

Now we need to look at the question, "Are you willing to be empty?" from the spiritual point of view. First of all, we *are* empty, whether we like it or not. Every atom in our body is composed of emptiness (more than 99 percent) inhabited by tiny bits of whizzing energy (less than 1 percent). In addition to our very real physical emptiness, we are empty in another way. We are empty of independent existence. We could not exist without all other beings also existing. Sometimes we become overwhelmed by the multitude of "others" and might wish that everything else in the world would disappear, but if that happened, we too would disappear. Fundamentally, we are made up of our interactions with all other beings. We are each like a soap bubble in the middle of a huge mass of soap bubbles. We are made up of nothing but emptiness and our intersections and interactions with all the other beings. And so are they.

To be willing to be empty is to align with a fundamental truth of our being.

Let's look at emptiness another way. We could frame the question thus: "Are you willing to do nothing? To sit or stand or lie down and do nothing?"

There is a natural rhythm that is characteristic of all life: the eternal cresting and ebbing of the ocean, the waxing and waning of the moon, the universal in-breath and out-breath of all living creatures, the steady beating of our hearts. Life depends upon this incessant alternation. If it were always night or if our heart could not relax after it contracts, life would end. The out-breath is as important as the in-breath. Emptying is as important as filling. We know this in relationship to our breath, but we've forgotten it in relationship to our stomach. We've also forgotten it in relation to our minds.

When we eat and drink all the time, our stomach and all our other digestive organs never get a rest. When we never let ourselves become truly hungry, our enjoyment of food decreases. Isn't it ironic? We think that by eating more we are enjoying eating more, but this is not true. It is when we allow ourselves to become truly hungry, and then take time to eat slowly and with attention, that we find the most enjoyment.

Similarly, when we think all the time, our minds never get a rest. Here, too, emptying is as important as filling. Life-changing insights arise out of a quiet, open mind. So do seminal scientific discoveries. Archimedes realized the principle of displacement as he entered that bath, Newton the force of gravity as he rested under an apple tree. The equation for relativity flashed into Einstein's mind as he idly watched a passing train. This is also how important spiritual insights arise, in the receptive space of a mind that is calm and aware. This emptying is the essence of centering prayer or meditation. God can't call in on a busy line.

Why does a quiet, empty mind frighten us? One reason is that we think our worth in life, even our survival, depends upon being productive, productive of thoughts. Actually, mental health, creativity, and productivity depend upon emptying and resting the mind, at least part of the time. So does our spiritual health.

Why does an empty mouth or stomach frighten us? Because we think our survival depends upon being full. Actually good health and a long life depend upon letting the mouth and stomach be empty and rest.[1] Tibetan doctors recommend dividing the stomach into fourths. One fourth is for food, two fourths are for liquids, and one fourth should remain empty. Again the question arises: *For the sake of our physical, mental, and spiritual health, are we willing to be empty?*

EXERCISE

Experiencing Emptiness in the Body and Mind

This exercise is on track 13 on the audio CD.

1. Sit in meditation in the morning, before you have had anything to eat or drink. (It is fine to brush your teeth or have a few sips of tea or water, but not a whole cup or glass.)
2. Bring awareness to the breath, wherever you feel the sensations of breathing most clearly.
3. Bring awareness to the body.

- Are there places in the body that feel empty?
- Are the sensations of emptiness pleasant, neutral, or unpleasant?
- Do any impulses arise to change the sensations of emptiness in the body?
- Are there places in the body that feel full?
- Are the sensations of fullness pleasant, neutral, or unpleasant?
- Do any impulses arise to change the sensations of fullness in the body?

4. Now bring awareness to the mind. Imagine the mind as a large, empty room. Thoughts naturally accumulate in this room like dry leaves blowing into an empty storehouse. You are interested in keeping this room clean and empty for a while.

Imagine the out-breath as a wind or a quiet leaf blower. The out-breath scatters thoughts as they accumulate and blows them out of the room. The room returns to its original state, empty and quiet.

Are the sensations of a mind that is empty like a great room pleasant, neutral, or unpleasant? Do any impulses arise to change the awareness of an empty mind?

Desires Are Inexhaustible

Many obvious desires arise within our mind in a single day: desire to sleep longer, to have a cup of coffee, to empty our bladder, to eat breakfast, to drive faster than the speed limit in order to get to work on time, or to not go to work at all. Less-blatant desires are more difficult to detect until we spend a day in quiet contemplation or meditation and some space opens up around our thoughts. We then can watch a parade of subtle desires in our mind: desire to laugh, desire to cough, desire to scratch, desire to have a donut, desire to move, desire to be still, desire for ice cream, desire for companionship. We can even watch the desire to think arise.

If everyone acted on all their desires, the world would be in chaos. Many people only keep their desires in check because of laws and threats of punishment. People who are more aware realize that it is their own duty to control their desires. Recognizing, controlling, and rechanneling desires are the essential tasks of a person who is consciously working to realize their own potential and who wishes to live in harmony both within this body and in the body of larger society. This applies whether they hope to realize their potential as a musician, an athlete, or an awakened being.

There is a line in one of our daily chants at the monastery: "Desires are inexhaustible. I vow to end them." This is one of the four great vows of the bodhisattva, a person committed to ending the suffering of all beings. But where would we be without desires? Desires keep us alive as individuals and as a species. Without desire for food and drink, we would die. Without the desire for intimacy, there would be no families, no communities. Without desire for sex, we would not die, but we would not have come into being at all; within about a hundred years the entire human race would die out. Without the desire to become enlightened, there would be no Buddha; without the desire for union with God, there would be no Christ, no Muhammad. Desire is not inherently bad or sinful. Desire is just an energy. Like any other energy, it can be used in wholesome or unwholesome ways.

The problem is not desire but whether we can recognize desire arising and direct its energy skillfully. When we are able to notice, pause, and then choose not to pursue an unhealthy desire, our conditioning gradually decreases and loosens its difficult hold upon us. We become able to notice desire but not be distracted by it. Thus, little by little, we become free of the prison of inexhaustible desires.

Desire Is Impermanent

Mindful eating also helps us become aware of the impermanence of desire. All desires arise, persist for awhile, and then fade away. The fading away could take seconds or weeks. Remember the Krispy-Kreme-donut-desire-window that opened in my mind? It seemed imperative at the time to obtain one, but within a few weeks that desire-window closed, and it has not opened again. I had a most compelling, large chocolate-desire-mind-window for many years, until chocolate began to cause burning blisters in my mouth. After many painful trials that desire-window closed and has not opened again. Over the last few years I have watched the desire for particular snack foods appear, grow intense, and fade away. A partial list includes black licorice, Japanese peanut crackers, red grapefruit, original Sun Chips, marzipan, egg custard, pepper-crusted brie on thin crackers, lotus-seed moon cakes, and See's caffe-latte lollipops. Just reading the list makes me smile at the absurdity of those temporary passions. When we observe again and again how last month's passion has become this year's disinterest or even revulsion, we can watch the phenomenon of new desires arising and not be sucked into them.

A woman who tried mindful eating for the first time in one of our workshops exclaimed afterward, "My mouth felt huge!" This is true. The areas of the brain that process sensation from the lips, tongue, and mouth are hugely out of proportion relative to the rest of the body (much bigger than the areas for the entire chest or back, for example). Our huge mouth is loaded with sense receptors, and it loves them to be stimulated. When our sense receptors are being stimulated we feel most alive. The intense pounding music of a rock band, the breath-stopping gasp of a dose of jalapeno, the heart-stopping jolt of a sudden plunge of the roller coaster, the adrenalin high of a horror movie or the pathos of a soap opera, the huge hit of sugar in a Big Gulp—we humans seek these kinds of thrills out. They reaffirm that we are alive.

The trouble comes when seeking out these intense experiences then provides the reason to *be* alive. Most people don't know why they are alive. They haven't considered what the essential purpose of their life is and how to accomplish it. They look to movies and soap operas for a model of what a "normal" human life should be like, and they find their own life pales in comparison to the intense emotional ups and downs and bizarre life events experienced by the people on the screen. Forgetting that these are actors who are walking their way through a script on a tacked-together stage set, people feel they must bring this same intensity to their lives or they will have failed at life.

We enjoy eating because we enjoy having our sense organs stimulated. Our eyes like to see food, our tongue likes tastes and textures, and even the ear likes the sounds of chewing crunchy things. Our mind also is considered a sense organ in Buddhism. This is a surprise to many people. It is a sense organ that gathers the input from the other sense organs, and it also perceives thought. The mind likes thoughts about food, it likes reading recipes, it likes anticipating the next meal or snack.

Problems arise when our body-heart-mind complex is not satisfied with a healthy amount of food or drink because it wants more stimulation, more pleasure. This is a fundamental issue in mindful eating. When we eat mindfully we recognize that while the mouth or the small mind are demanding more sense pleasure, or the painful heart wants more soothing, the rest of our being has a choice about what we do with those demands.

The Buddha called this process "taming." Taming does not mean rigid control. The Buddha tried rigid control with food and almost starved to death. In his earlier life he had tried the opposite, a life of indulgence in sense pleasures including food. This did not lead to health and happiness either. He advised the wisdom of the middle way. The middle way is not a straight, easy road. We wobble along it, leaning to one side and then the other. When we lose our balance and veer off, mindfulness helps us realize what has happened so we can adjust our course.

How does the middle way apply to eating and food? It teaches that extremes are unskillful and will not bring the ease in life that we are looking for. It advises that rigid control and self-denial will not be healthy and will not lead to happiness. Neither will indulging our desires and always doing what is pleasurable. The one side (strict control and self-denial) is represented by anorexia, bulimia, and purging. The other side (overindulgence in pleasure) is represented by overeating and binging. There is a middle way with food. It is not static, a fixed set of rules. To apply to the changing circumstances of a human life it must be dynamic, flexible.

This might seem difficult at first. It might seem easier to follow black-and-white rules such as "Never eat sugar" or "Always eat what you crave." Sometimes sugar is appropriate to eat. Sometimes we shouldn't eat what we feel like eating.

It takes a while to learn to navigate our way down the path of the middle way. We need a compass pointing toward health and happiness, a map of spiritual teachings, a group to support us, and a guide. Above all we need mindfulness.

EXERCISE

Watching Desires

Become aware of desire for food and drink throughout the day. For example, when you get up in the morning, is desire already present? If not, when does it first arise in the mind?

Become aware of the stronger desires ("I have to have cup of coffee right now!") and the weaker ones (the thought of getting pizza on the way home makes a brief pass through your mind during a business meeting).

Create a gap by postponing acting on at least one desire for food or drink. Watch how long the desire persists, and see whether it grows stronger or weaker.

Be mindful of how desires arise in the mind, persist, and eventually disappear.

Eating Can Be a Sacred Activity

Once I led a group of religious leaders in the exercise of eating one raisin mindfully. Afterward a Catholic priest approached me. He wanted to describe his experience of eating the raisin, of his mouth flooding with sensation and his entire being flooding with joy. Tears glinting in his eyes, he said, "This is how the Communion wafer has always been for me, since my First Communion as a boy. It is an amazing mystery. How can one small bit of food be full of so many subtle and lasting flavors, so completely satisfying!"

This is the miracle of the fishes and loaves, that a crumb of bread and a single sip of wine can expand and satisfy the hunger of many people. It is not a particular food, even a blessed food, that is the key to this kind of satisfaction. Anything can unlock it: a falling plum blossom, the taste of a single blackberry, the smell of burning leaves, a sudden shaft of light piercing through a mass of dark clouds, the words of a Jewish carpenter or a Indian wanderer. When something opens the channel between our heart and the holy mystery that is present in every moment of our life, then we are fed from the source of deepest truth. If this happens when we are eating, then physical food becomes spiritual food.

The food we eat contains the life force of innumerable creatures, brought to us that we might have life and have it more abundantly. The myriad beings of all of creation are always offering us a life of abundance, but we are most often unaware of it. The Catholic ritual of Communion, the Zen ritual of *oryoki*, can make us present, opening our senses to that great Presence. When we are open, a bit of matzo or a single shriveled raisin can transform not only our experience of eating but our entire experience of what it is to be alive.

As a young adult I found the teaching in the church of my childhood opaque. I was not satisfied to sit in the pews and hear words about God. I wanted the actual experience of God's presence. I could feel it, tantalizingly close, just on the other side of a thin curtain. My Zen teachers offered me a way to lift that curtain, a way that was available not just to a select few but to everyone. I signed up for a weeklong silent Zen retreat and, the first night, was instructed in the ritual of *oryoki*. I began following every moment of eating as mindfully as I could. One day, as I swallowed some juice, I traced its path into the mouth, down the throat, and into my body, into the cells, down to the toes. Suddenly I was overwhelmed by the continuous experience of coming-into-union. This was Communion, hidden in plain sight, hidden in the food, in my mouth and body, and in the scriptures, all along!

In Zen we call something that has the potential to awaken us to a deeper truth about our life a "dharma gate." Every evening at the monastery we chant, "Dharma gates are boundless. I vow to enter them." Why are dharma gates boundless? Because they are everywhere. Anything can be a gate to a deeper truth, if we are able to sit perfectly still and truly open to it. Actually there is no gate at all, but our confused and distracted minds present us with a convincing illusion of walls with gates that are closed, blocking our access to Eden's garden. "True nature" is wide open and always apparent. However, from this, the everyday side of things, we see numberless gates. When we do anything with awareness, we increase the potential that these dharma gates will open. When a dharma gate opens, we are able to have many experiences that we long for but that ordinarily elude us: experiences of the sacred, intimacy, oneness, abundance, gratitude, well-being, and simple happiness. Eating can be called sacred because it can become, through mindful eating, a dependable dharma gate.

We all eat and drink, at least several times a day. This means that no matter what else is happening in our busy lives, we have several chances a day to enter a place of inquiry, a place of renewal, a place of simple happiness. When we are able to find happiness in the most basic activities of our lives—breathing, walking, eating, drinking, and lying down to sleep—we discover an ancient secret, the secret of how to become truly happy and at ease in our lives. I hope you'll continue to experiment with the mindfulness practices presented in this book and discover new worlds of pleasure, abundance, and gratitude—all of which are lying unfalteringly within the drink in your cup and the food on your plate.

SHIP
TO: Eilene Okerblom
1014 Fairway Vista Dr
Santa Maria CA 93455
United States Of America

ORDER NO.	PAGE NO.
88749A1013191	1

SHIPMENT NO.
6916895

SHIP VIA	DATE
USPS DELIVERY CONFIR	3/16/09

TEXTBOOKX.com
25 Van Zant Street
Norwalk, CT 06855

Item Number	SHIP	Line	Item Description	Ord	Purchase Order No.
9781590305317	1	001	MINDFUL EATING A GUIDE TO REDISCOVERING	1	1
9781590304150	1	002	PARTNERS IN HEALING SIMPLE WAYS TO OFFER	1	1
	2	...	TOTAL QUANTITY FOR ORDER ...	2	2
			END OF ORDER 3/16/09 15:38:53		

Reason for return:_____

Textbookx.com Returns
25 Van Zant Street
Norwalk, CT 06855

VIA: MDC
SHIPPER NO. XXXX
PKG. ID#
91020293683052247I4224

Return Label

ORDER # 88749A1013191

Eilene Okerblom
1014 Fairway Vista Dr
Santa Maria CA 93455
United States Of America

TextbookX.com
25 Van Zant street
Norwalk, CT 06855

6916895

Eilene Okerblom
1014 Fairway Vista Dr
Santa Maria CA 93455

TextbookX.com
25 Van Zant Street
Norwalk, CT 06855

718525366 - 304

Summary Tips

IN THIS BOOK we've explored a great deal of information and practices. Here's a quick review of the essential points. It might be helpful to return to this list from time to time, as you work to make mindful eating part of your everyday life.

- Mindful eating is about opening the mind's awareness to our food and to the body, before, during, and after we eat.
- Mindful eating is nonjudgmental.
- Awareness is the key to change. Once we are aware of something, it cannot remain the same. Awareness plus small changes in our automatic behaviors can produce large changes over time.
- Learn to assess stomach and cellular hunger before you eat, during eating, and after eating.
- If you are not hungry, don't eat.
- Be present for at least the first three bites or sips as you begin to eat or drink.
- Eat small portions, considering "right amount." Serve yourself an amount of food that will leave you two-thirds full.
- Eat slowly, savoring each bite. Find ways of pausing as you eat, such as putting down your fork or spoon between bites.
- Chew your food thoroughly before swallowing.
- Become aware of the difference between "no longer hungry" and

"full." There is no need to eat all the way to "full." Eat until you are two-thirds full, then take a drink and rest a bit.

- Mindful eating includes mindless eating. You can choose to eat mindlessly when it is appropriate.
- Emptying is as important as filling. This applies both to the stomach and to the mind.
- At least once a week, eat an entire meal in silence and mindfulness.
- Know that food changes mood and use it as good medicine. Adjust the dose; a small amount may work better than a lot.
- Remember the energy equation: balance the energy going into your body with the energy going out.
- Above all, know when it is not the body but the heart that is asking to be fed. Give it the nutrition that fills it up. That nutrition could be meditation or prayer, walking, being in nature, listening to or making music, playing with a pet, fixing food for someone you love or who needs help, or just sitting and being present with people. Fill the heart with the richness of this very moment.
- Before, during, and after eating, give thanks.

DEDICATION OF MERIT

IN THE BUDDHIST TRADITION, we conclude periods of teaching and meditation practice with a short dedication of merit in which we express our aspiration that the work we've done be of benefit not only to ourselves, but to all beings. In that spirit,

May we all become free from anxiety and fear about eating. May we all be at ease. May we all be content as we nourish this precious human body and mind. May our hearts be happy and satisfied as we walk the path of awakening.

NOTES

Chapter 1: What Is Mindful Eating?

1. For a bibliography of research on the benefits of mindfulness-based stress reduction, see www.umassmed.edu/Content.aspx?id=42066.

Chapter 2: The Seven Kinds of Hunger

1. Brian Wansink, *Mindless Eating: Why We Eat More Than We Think* (New York: Bantam, 2006), pp. 15–19.

2. Ibid., pp. 46–52.

3. Ibid., pp. 120–121.

4. Ibid., pp. 65–68 and 178–179.

5. Ibid., pp. 111–112.

6. Michael Pollan, "Our National Eating Disorder," *The New York Times Magazine*, October 17, 2004.

7. Daniel M. Bernstein, Cara Laney, Erin K. Morris, and Elizabeth F. Loftus, "False Beliefs about Fattening Foods Can Have Healthy Consequences," *Proceedings of the National Academy of Sciences* 102, no. 39 (September 27, 2005): 13724–13731.

8. An article by Susan Casey, "Plastic Ocean" (www.bestlifeonline.com/cms/publish/travel-leisure/Our_oceans_are_turning_into_plastic_are_we.shtml), describes the dangers in haunting detail. See also Matt McGowan, "Uncovering Hidden Danger" (http://atmizzou.missouri.edu/juno3/plastics.html), which describes the research of Frederick vom Saal.

9. Wansink, pp. 104–105.

10. Myrna Goldenberg, "Cookbooks and Concentration Camps: Unlikely Partners" (www.jewishvirtuallibrary.org/jsource/Holocaust/cookbook.html). A related story is documented by Cara de Silva, *In Memory's Kitchen: A Legacy from the Women of Terezin* (Northvale, N.J.: Aronson, 1996). Elizabeth Farnsworth

interviewed de Silva about the book for *The NewsHour with Jim Lehrer* on December 17, 1996 (transcript available online at www.pbs.org/newshour/bb/europe/december96/cook_12-17.html).

11. Song of Survival, a video documentary about the women prisoners in Sumatra, produced in 2004 by Veriation Films, was developed from a radio documentary by the same name; see Roger Emanuels, http://baymoon.com/~emanuels/sofs.html. The story is also told in Helen Colijn, *Song of Survival: Women Interned* (Ashland, Ore.: White Cloud Press, 1995).

Chapter 3: Exploring Our Habits and Patterns with Food

1. Brian Wansink, *Mindless Eating: Why We Eat More Than We Think* (New York: Bantam, 2006), pp. 100–102.

2. Ibid., pp. 156–159.

3. Amy J. Sindler, Nancy S. Wellman, and Oren Baruch Stier, "Holocaust Survivors Report Long-Term Effects on Attitudes toward Food," *Journal of Nutritional Education and Behavior* 36, no. 4 (July 2004): 189–196.

Chapter 4: Six Simple Guidelines for Mindful Eating

1. Dallas Bogan, "Foods of the Early Tavern and Household," *History of Campbell County, Tennessee* (www.tngenweb.org/campbell/hist-bogan/tavernfood.html).

2. Brian Wansink, *Mindless Eating: Why We Eat More Than We Think* (New York: Bantam, 2006), p. 46.

3. Gina Kolata, "Maybe You're *Not* What You Eat," *The New York Times*, February 14, 2006.

4. "First Research Confirms That Eating Slowly Inhibits Appetite," November 15, 2006, www.physorg.com/news82810846.html.

5. Martha T. Conklin and Laurel G. Lambert, "Eating at School: A Summary of NFSMI Research on Time Required by Students to Eat Lunch," National Food Service Management Institute, University of Mississippi, April 2001 (www.schoolwellnesspolicies.org/resources/eating_at_school.pdf).

6. Anand Vaishnav, "School Lunches Are No Picnic: Longer Student Breaks Are Advocated," *The Boston Globe*, August 6, 2005.

7. Kellie Patrick, "Just No Time to Enjoy Lunch: More and More the Midday Meal Is a Student Option," *The Philadelphia Inquirer*, November 28, 2006.

8. Wansink, p. 80.

9. National Catholic Rural Life Conference, www.ncrlc.com.

10. Ajahn Chah, *Food for the Heart: Collected Teachings of Ajahn Chah* (Boston: Wisdom, 2002), p. 236.

11. Lisa R. Young and Marion Nestle, "The Contribution of Expanding Portion

Sizes to the U.S. Obesity Epidemic," *American Journal of Public Health* 92, no. 2 (2002): 246–249.

12. Wansink, p. 59.

13. Ibid., pp. 66–68 and 175–177. See also Centers for Disease Control, National Center for Chronic Disease Prevention and Health Promotion, "Do Increased Portion Sizes Affect How Much We Eat?" Research to Practice Series No. 2, May 2006. (http://www.cdc.gov/nccdphp/dnpa/nutrition/pdf/portion_size_research.pdf.)

14. Lisa R. Young and Marion Nestle, "The Contribution of Expanding Portion Sizes to the U.S. Obesity Epidemic," *American Journal of Public Health* 92, no. 2 (2002): 246–249.

15. Centers for Disease Control, National Center for Chronic Disease Prevention and Health Promotion, "Do Increased Portion Sizes Affect How Much We Eat?" Research to Practice Series No. 2, May 2006. See also B.J. Rolls, D. Engel, L.L. Birch, "Serving Portion Size Influences 5-Year-Olds But Not 3-Year-Old Children's Food Intakes," *Journal of the American Dietetic Association* 100 (2000): 232–234.

16. Centers for Disease Control, National Center for Chronic Disease Prevention and Health Promotion, "Do Increased Portion Sizes Affect How Much We Eat?" Research to Practice Series No. 2, May 2006.

17. Yatsutani Roshi, "Precautions to Observe in Zazen," in *The Three Pillars of Zen: Teaching, Practice, Enlightenment*, edited by Philip Kapleau (Boston: Beacon Press, 1967), pp. 36–37.

18. Wansink, pp. 78–79.

19: Ibid., p. 80.

20. See research cited in John Tierney, "Comfort Food, for Monkeys," *New York Times Science Times*, May 20, 2008, pp. 1 and 6.

21. One relevant study is E. Epel, et al, " Are Stress Eaters at Risk for the Metabolic Syndrome?" *Annals of the New York Academy of Sciences* 1032 (Dec. 2004): 208–210.

22. For a larger discussion see Hal Stone and Sidra Stone, *Embracing Your Inner Critic: Turning Self Criticism into a Creative Asset* (San Francisco: HarperSanFrancisco, 1993).

Chapter 5: Cultivating Gratitude

1. Rozin, P. C. Fischler, S. Imada, A. Sarubin, and A. Wrzesniewski, "Attitudes to Food and the Role of Food in Life in the U.S.A., Japan, Flemish Belgium, and France: Possible Implications for the Diet–Health Debate," *Appetite* 33, no. 2 (1999): 163–180.

2. Bhikkhu Nanamoli, trans., and Bhikkhu Bodhi, trans. and ed., *The Middle*

Length Discourses of the Buddha: A New Translation of the Majjhima Nikaya (Boston: Wisdom, 1995). Sutta 10, "The Four Foundations of Mindfulness." "Body as body" is the first in a set of practices called the four foundations of mindfulness. It is followed by mindfulness of feelings as feelings (more subtle than emotions, more like a feeling tone), mindfulness of the ground of mind, and mindfulness of the objects that float in and out of the mind's awareness.

3. There are a number of variations on the body scan. One teacher in the Tibetan tradition has students imagine a glowing, green, beneficial liquid that gradually fills up the body, carrying away all afflictions as it spills out through the pores and overflows the top of the head.

4. Norman Waddell, trans., *Wild Ivy: The Spiritual Autobiography of Zen Master Hakuin* (Boston: Shambhala, 1999), pp. 105–107.

Chapter 6: Conclusion

1. Studies show that calorie restriction prolongs life in many animals and has clear health benefits in humans. For example, see Washington University School of Medicine, "Calorie Restriction Appears Better Than Exercise at Slowing Primary Aging," *Science Daily*, May 31, 2006 (www.sciencedaily.com/releases/2006/05/060531164818.htm).

RESOURCES

Organizations

The Center for Mindfulness in Medicine, Health Care, and Society at the University of Massachusetts Medical School Founded by Dr. Jon Kabat-Zinn, who has been a pioneer in bringing mindfulness to mainstream medicine and society, the center sponsors an annual conference featuring research on mindfulness-based stress reduction (MBSR), including the use of MBSR in eating disorders. See www.umassmed.edu.

The Center for Mindful Eating (TCME) A forum for professionals interested in mindful eating, TCME identifies and provides resources for professionals who wish to help their clients develop healthier relationships with food and eating and bring eating into balance with other important aspects of life. The Center for Mindful Eating does not promote one single approach to mindful eating but is committed to dialog and the sharing of ideas, clinical experience, and research. See www.tcme.org.

Books and Additional Sources

Albers, Susan. *Eating Mindfully: How to End Mindless Eating and Enjoy a Balanced Relationship with Food.* Oakland, Calif.: New Harbinger, 2003. This book contains many useful skill-building exercises based upon the Buddhist teaching of the Four Foundations of Mindfulness. See more at www.eatingmindfully.com.

Altman, Donald. *Art of the Inner Meal: Foods for Thought and Spiritual Eating*. Los Angeles: Moon Lake Media, 1998. This book focuses on the spiritual basis of mindful eating in many religious traditions and includes a number of practical exercises. See more at www.mindful practices.com.

Gerrard, Don. *One Bowl: A Guide to Eating for Body and Spirit*. New York: Marlowe & Company, 2001. A guide to a strikingly simple way to eat mindfully and nourish body and spirit by using one bowl.

Goodall, Jane. *Harvest for Hope: A Guide to Mindful Eating*. New York: Warner, 2005. A call to make a difference by learning where our food comes from and how our choices in eating can have profound effects upon us, other beings, and the earth. See more at www.janegoodall.com.

Kabatznick, Ronna. *Zen of Eating: Ancient Answers to Modern Weight Problems*. New York: Berkeley, 1998. Written by a long-time meditator who also is a psychologist specializing in weight management, this book shows how the fundamental teachings of the Buddha, the Four Noble Truths and the Eightfold Path, can be applied to disordered eating.

National Catholic Rural Life Conference. "Eating Is a Moral Act." Offers principles of and insights into the ethics of eating. Offers a series of cards on topics including the Eater's Bill of Rights, the dignity of farmers and farm workers, and the web of life. Text available at www.ncrlc.com/cards.htm.

Roth, Geneen. *Feeding the Hungry Heart: The Experience of Compulsive Eating*. New York: Plume, 1993; *When You Eat at the Refrigerator, Pull Up a Chair: 50 Ways to Be Thin, Gorgeous, and Happy When You Feel Anything But*. New York: Hyperion, 1998. Roth has written a number of books on eating disorders in a witty, personal, and inspirational style. A central theme is how to recognize the heart's hunger and nourish it in appropriate ways. See more at www.geneenroth.com.

Tribole, Evelyn, and Elyse Resch. *Intuitive Eating: A Revolutionary Program That Works.* Rev. ed. New York: St. Martin's Griffin, 2003. A book about how to eat guided by information from the body rather than succumbing to the counterproductive, confused, and critical mind. See more at www.intuitiveeating.com.

United States Conference of Catholic Bishops. Statement issued in 2003: "For I Was Hungry and You Gave Me Food." Reflections on solving hunger in the human family, on ensuring dignity for farmers, and on preserving God's creation. Text available at www.usccb.org/bishops/agricultural.shtml

Wansink, Brian. *Mindless Eating: Why We Eat More Than We Think.* New York: Bantam, 2006. A fascinating compilation of the research on how and why our eating is directed by environmental clues and conditioning. This book is very funny but also sobering, when you realize that you eat the same mindless way as the folks in these experiments. See more at www.mindlesseating.com.

INDEX

obesity, epidemic of, xi
oils, changing fads and, 45
Okinawans, and "eight parts full," 105
oryoki (Zen ceremony of eating just enough), 103
out of sight, out of mind, in mindful eating, 112–117

pacifiers, 64
pausing, while eating, 100
Pavlov's experiments, 63, 65–66
perfectionist, the inner, 118
pica (eating disorder), 41
plastic water containers, 48
Pollan, Michael, 46
portion sizes
  and the "appestat" in children, 104–105
  huge increases in, 104
  in other countries, 104, 105
  and plate, bowl, and serving utensil sizes, 21
  in restaurants, 17
  supersizing, xi
  See also right amount
pusher, the inner, 119

questions about mindful eating, 127–129

raisin meditations
  basic mindful eating meditation, 11–13
  looking deeply into our food exercise, 140–141
research on eating
  appetite, and the perception of masculinity (Brad on a date), 65
  the bottomless soup bowl, 21
  calorie intake, and eating speed, 97
  children and portion size, 105
  concentration camp survivors, 56, 71
  cross-cultural attitudes toward food, 131
  implanting false memories of food likes and dislikes, 47
  mindfulness-based stress reduction, benefits of, 3

order in which people eat food, 69
portion sizes, 21, 104–105
school lunch, time allotted for, 98–99
secretaries and chocolates, 113
stale popcorn, and the power of the eyes, 21
resources, 165–167
restaurant eating, and eye hunger, 20–21
right amount, in mindful eating, 102–106

sacred activity, eating as, 153–155
salt
  depletion, 39–40
  as essential nutrient, 85, 89–90
satiety
  in children, 104–105
  relying on visual cues for, 67–68
  and slower eating, 96–102
scents, and hunger. *See* nose hunger
school cafeteria eating, 98–99
scientific studies. *See* research on eating
seasonal aspects of cellular hunger, 41–42, 107
self-soothing with food, 66
seven types of hunger, 12–13, 18–62
  See also cellular hunger; eye hunger; heart hunger; mind hunger; mouth hunger; nose hunger; stomach hunger, sitting meditation practice
slowing down, in mindful eating, 92–103
smell, sense of, and hunger. *See* nose hunger
snacking, 143–145
"soft butter meditation," Hakuin Zenji's, 135–136
soothing oneself with food, 66
speed of eating, American, 93–94
spoon, putting down between bites, 101
spring water vs. tap water, 48
starvation
  fear of, 77–78
  stories of, 78–81
  working with fear of, 82–84
stomach hunger, 12–13, 34–38

ABOUT THE AUTHOR

JAN CHOZEN BAYS, MD, is a pediatrician, a Zen teacher, wife, mother, and grandmother. She has studied and practiced Zen since 1973 and has taught mindful eating for more than twenty years to individuals and healthcare professionals.

Dr. Bays is currently on staff at Legacy Children's Hospital in Portland, Oregon. She received her Zen training under the revered Zen master Taizan Maezumi Roshi and then under Shodo Harada Roshi, abbot of Sogen-ji monastery in Japan. She is the coabbot of the Great Vow Zen Monastery in Clatskanie, Oregon, and the author of the book *Jizo Bodhisattva.*

For more information, visit www.mindfuleatingbook.com.

LIST OF CD TRACKS

Running time: 1 hour 15 minutes